THE
FINAL
DEADLINE

*What Death Has
Taught Me about Life*

Other books by Chris Glaser:

As My Own Soul
The Blessing of Same-Gender Marriage

Uncommon Calling
A Gay Christian's Struggle to Serve the Church

Come Home!
Reclaiming Spirituality and Community as Gay Men and Lesbians

Coming Out to God
Prayers for Lesbians and Gay Men, Their Families and Friends

The Word Is Out
Daily Reflections on the Bible for Lesbians and Gay Men

Coming Out as Sacrament

Reformation of the Heart
Seasonal Meditations by a Gay Christian

Unleashed
The Wit and Wisdom of Calvin the Dog

Communion of Life
Meditations for the New Millennium

Henri's Mantle
100 Meditations on Nouwen's Legacy

Troy Perry
Pastor and Prophet

THE
FINAL
DEADLINE

What Death Has
Taught Me about Life

CHRIS GLASER

Dear
Chris
&
Anne —
Great
to see
you again!
Love,
Chris
Atlanta
Oct 26
2010

Morehouse Publishing
NEW YORK · HARRISBURG · DENVER

Unless otherwise noted, the Scripture quotations contained herein are from the New Revised Standard Version Bible, copyright © 1989 by the Division of Christian Education of the National Council of Churches of Christ in the U.S.A. Used by permission. All rights reserved.

Morehouse Publishing, 4775 Linglestown Road, Harrisburg, PA 17112

Morehouse Publishing, 445 Fifth Avenue, New York, NY 10016

Morehouse Publishing is an imprint of Church Publishing Incorporated.
www.churchpublishing.org

Cover design by Laurie Klein Westhafer

Typeset by MediaLynx

Library of Congress Cataloging-in-Publication Data

Glaser, Chris.
    The final deadline : what death has taught me about life / Chris R. Glaser.
       p. cm.
    ISBN 978-0-8192-2378-4 (pbk.)
    ISBN 978-0-8192-2729-4 (Ebook)
    ISBN 978-0-8192-2736-2 (Kindle)
1. Death--Religious aspects--Christianity. I. Title.
    BT825.G53 2010
    236'.1--dc22

                            2010008692

Printed in the United States of America

10 11 12 13 14 15   10 9 8 7 6 5 4 3 2 1

◎

*To all who have gone before
and have shown me the way,*

*especially Scott Rogo,
Tommy Thompson,
and of course,
Calvin.*

◎

Contents

Acknowledgments

Thanks to publisher Davis Perkins, acquiring editor Susan Erdey, and the editorial board at Church Publishing for encouraging me in this writing endeavor. I am very grateful to Frank Tedeschi for his enthusiasm for my writing and his conscientious work as editor. Thanks to copyeditor Dennis Ford for helping me be clear to the reader.

Thanks to cover designer Laurie Klein Westhafer and book designer Denise Hoff at MediaLynx, for their creativity in the look of this book, and to proofreader Cliffy Shiner for saving us from textual mistakes. Thanks to all who market, distribute, and sell this book. All of these are the unsung saints of the publishing business.

Thanks to my family members for their support—my partner, Wade Jones, and our dog, Hobbes.

Thanks to you the reader for considering not only what Death has taught me, but what it teaches all of us about living life deeply and mindfully.

I thank all whose deaths I contemplate in this book and the many more not mentioned who have contributed their lives to the human enterprise, and in so doing, have prompted my own spiritual growth. In life, there is no such thing as a "self-made" man or woman.

Finally, I thank God for making us as we are with all our limits and possibilities.

Chris Glaser
Atlanta, Georgia

Chapter ONE
A Friendly Deadline

"You have more dead friends than Jessica Fletcher," a longtime friend once told me, referring to the Maine mystery writer of the *Murder She Wrote* television series. He was dead on, so to speak. I have so many friends on "the other side" that, at times, crossing over seems friendlier than it once did. At other times death seems terrifying, especially if it might be premature or "my own fault" or worse, before fulfilling some dream or vision. "I'd rather be waiting to die than waiting to live," I once wrote to myself. What I meant was that too often we postpone life, as if there were no deadline.

As a writer and editor, I have come to experience deadlines as friendly. I don't mean friendly in the sense of "soft" deadlines, but friendly in the knowledge that such and such a time requires having accomplished the goal of finishing an article, a book, or "putting to bed" an issue of a magazine. Most editors know that if you assign a writer an article with no deadline you are less likely to receive the article at all, unless the writer herself imposes her own deadline. So why not view death as the final deadline, one that insists we "get it" or "get it done" (whatever "it" is) during our lifetime?

As the ultimate deadline, death has taught me much about life. Death is an inscrutable, puzzling, and even stern Zen master ready to teach me whenever I am ready to learn. Death is a spiritual director for those with eyes to see and ears to hear, hearts to feel and minds to know. Death is the friendly opposition on whose rough headstone we hone our blade of life—a defining edge, as it were. Death is a soul-friend who shadows us all our lives and will be there with us at the end. My spiritual training and experience keep me mindful of all the ways by which God and the universe unveil what is vital—life-giving—even death itself.

Our religious traditions often attempt to shield us from death, promising eternal life, denying or demeaning physical existence, viewing earthly life simply as a "test" for "the real thing"—whether that real thing is some grander, heavenly existence, or what remains after we are delivered from the illusion of the material world. Death is variously viewed as a moral, natural, or necessary evil, a punishment for original sin or for thinking negative thoughts, a passageway to the kingdom of heaven or Nirvana, a resurrection or rebirth, or a deliverance from rebirth. "Go toward the light," has become a cliché in our time. I myself have written of death as a threshold.

But to write of death as a threshold implies a doorway and a door, a door closed or slammed in the face of all we know and leave behind. Beyond what we know lie belief and faith, valuable resources in life. But life is more than belief and faith: life is here and now, day by day, love and hate, pleasure and pain, joy and suffering, success and failure. Existentialism has served as a corrective to our complex methods of denial that we each must die—and thus also a denial that we each must live, *now.* Nihilism and the pseudo-nihilism embraced by culturally alternative black-clothed, mostly young people (nihilism as "style") appear to embrace the opposite: that we must die, *now,* in the midst of life— that our lives, in a sense, must be infected or infested with death, that whatever we accomplish is somehow diminished or defeated by death (So "why bother?").

My spiritual mentor Henri Nouwen believed that the fear of death leads to many if not most of our personal and societal ills. Using Jungian insight, influenced by James Hillman, he spoke of "befriending" death. So I write in the pages that follow of death as a friendly spiritual guide, a kindly if awesome teacher about what is vital, important, and ultimate. Death's lessons for me may echo its lessons for you, or bring to mind other lessons that your death experience has given you. Just as schools may give credit for what is called "life experience," so death experience may serve as an accredited course in the spiritual life, but only if we attend its lectures, study its texts, and reflect on its applications to life.

While writing this book I was invited to lead a workshop at a progressive men's spirituality conference. I was aware that working on this book had dredged up all kinds of grief, not just about death, but about life. I had had a dream in which I was working in a morgue, conducting autopsies of incomplete bodies that came in cardboard clothing boxes. I told my dream to a therapist friend whom I periodically meet for lunch, and I asked him what he thought of it. "Sounds like it has something to do with whatever motivation is prompting you to write this book," he said simply. Thus I was eager to hear the presentation on grief of a plenary speaker at the men's conference. But the speaker's talk did not connect to my experience, though I so very much wanted it to do so. On a feeling level, he made me vaguely uncomfortable—not because of the subject matter, but because he reminded me of a member of a church I served of whom we used to joke, "If so-and-so comes to visit you, you know you're dying." She was the Emmeline Grangerford of our congregation. You might recall that character from Mark Twain's *Adventures of Huckleberry Finn*, the fourteen-year-old girl who wrote poems for the dead, often arriving at the death-site before the undertaker. As this presenter at the men's gathering announced (proudly? self-satisfied?) that as a hospice worker he had accompanied four hundred people to their deaths, I wondered more at the health of his inclination to do so and his keeping count than at the number, then questioned my own inclination to write this book. Was I claiming some sort of "bragging rights" about the deaths I had experienced? Am I trying to gain sympathy for my "woundedness"? Am I just a grown-up version of Emmeline Grangerford, writing prosaic odes to the dead in a kind of morbid preoccupation?

The reader may judge otherwise, but I have acquitted myself because I know myself too well. First of all I have practiced the very human trait of avoidance, not so much of talking about death but of being around death itself. I've only been around death because that was my job, either as a friend, a family member, a volunteer, or a minister. I kept careful boundaries in terms of my involvement, even during the AIDS pandemic, to keep myself from possible morbidity or burnout by becoming overly focused on death and dying. And I never counted, especially my friends who died of AIDS, because my friends were not to be treated as statistics. Ironically, though the speaker on grief did not help me with my own, during a break I learned of the unusual death of yet another friend which I will recount in a later chapter. That story will stay with me longer than anything the hospice worker said. Grief lingers longer than any attempt at cure.

I was stunned by a friend in college who announced that he had just attended his first funeral. He said he came out of the church and saw the shining sun and blue sky as if for the first time, and smiled grandly and thankfully in response. The experience made him want to fully embrace life, the central teaching of death, in my view. My surprise came from hearing that he had never been to a funeral before. My parents never shielded me from death. As protective as my mother was of her children, I don't think it even occurred to her that children should not go to funerals.

My first encounter with death was that of my maternal grandmother when I was five or six years of age. It revealed the terror and grief death brings, as well as its homeliness and familiarity. We lived in California and most of our relatives lived in the heart of the United States: Kansas, Missouri, Oklahoma, and Texas. The report of family deaths always seemed to come by way of early morning phone calls. For years, I came to associate early morning phone calls with death, especially if my mother picked up the phone, because she would stare blankly (pensively?) into space in silence for what seemed an eternity, attentive to the voice on the other end of the line, and my heart would begin beating rapidly as I awaited another pronouncement of death. My brother felt the same way, and when my mother would answer, "No, we already subscribe to the paper," or "No, we don't want to take another magazine," we would breathe sighs of relief, but then, annoyed, take my mother to task for frightening us by her deer-in-the-headlights look. She did not do this on purpose, though she did play a game that could be considered cruel by today's entirely too fastidious child-rearing standards. As a practical joker, she would play dead occasionally, and I remember panicking a little each time, fearing she was not pretending, shaking her vigorously to get her to move and laugh and open her eyes, which she invariably did. That is, of course, until the day she actually died. All of us were practical jokers in the family, perhaps (for us children at least) an Irish trait we inherited from our mother's side, sometimes a little sick or twisted but always intended in good fun. This also gave us leeway to withdraw a stinging remark by claiming, "I was only joking." So when my brother, the family's master of practical jokes, called to tell me decades later that Mom had passed away, my first inclination was to say, disbelievingly, "You're kidding." Fortunately, I held my tongue. But I am getting ahead of my story.

I can't recall whether the phone call about my grandmother came early in the morning, but I do remember my father being there (called home from work?) and my mother screaming her pain and her grief in their bedroom early one morning, collapsing, sobbing, on the bed and then the floor, cursing the doctors who had treated her mother, blaming herself for not being there. This prompted me to declare to my brother and sister in all five-year-old seriousness, "I'm going to kill those doctors when we get there!" They shamed me with the stock reply of elders that I was too young to know what I was talking about.

Over the years, my grandmother had been in and out of Mt. Carmel hospital, the Catholic hospital in her small hometown of Pittsburg, Kansas, with a mystery ailment so serious that my mother, the eldest of five, had to quit college to oversee the family. Her family was Baptist, not Catholic, but the nuns were very good to my grandmother and her brood of Protestant heretics. My grandmother had made a quilt for one of the sisters to show her gratitude for her care. My mother also seemed quite fond of the sisters, and, an inveterate reader, took their tips on Catholic writers to read at a time when Baptists and Catholics were condemning one another from their respective pulpits. The spiritual practice of the quilt recipient required her not to accept the gift directly, as I recall, but first to use it for a patient until the latter expired. "Expired" was a curious term for me as a child, making me wonder why we don't have "expiration dates" on us like packaged food, but less puzzling when contrasted with "inspired," that is, breath breathed into the first human being.

The immediate great regret of my mother was that she had not phoned her mother the Sunday before. Long-distance phone calls were a costly rarity in those days, especially for our family of modest income, and, of course, most were placed on weekends when rates were lowest. My father had persuaded her they couldn't afford it that week—I would think a source of recrimination toward him later, though I never heard my mother say that, then or ever, though she would explain this as the case matter-of-factly rather than accusingly, maybe recrimination enough. Perhaps, behind their closed bedroom door (always a sign that they were intimately engaged), or, more hidden still, within her heart, she did. I say that because I would have, but then, I've grown up in a litigious culture that blames everyone else but one's self. Ultimately, being a good Christian, she blamed herself. She was the one who moved so far away for the great love of her life, my dad, and she would have a taste of that experience when I did the same during the final years of her life. She would remind herself then (and be reminded by her sisters) that she had done that very thing long ago, and she would tell me so to assure me that it was the right thing to do. Unfortunately, her love lasted longer than that of my "great love," but again, I'm getting ahead of my story.

No one in my family flew in those days, except my adventurous and independent Aunt Helen. We drove everywhere, and it was my father who did the driving, given that he was a professional sales driver for Weber's bread, and the fact that my mother never learned to drive. We drove the three-day trip to Kansas for the funeral, and I remember getting out of the car and seeing my Aunt Ann and Aunt Grace outside the family home to greet us, and the youngest, Aunt Grace, I think, embracing my mother, both in tears.

Being young and impressionable, I overheard a conversation about what I thought was a man's death at the funeral home, so when my father lifted me up to see my grandmother in her coffin, I did not recognize the kind and gentle stocky woman who had given me during my last visit a throw rug that I had liked; I thought it was the man they had talked about. Death does transform us into something not entirely like ourselves, which argues for the existence of something we cannot see: a soul, a spirit, an enlivening presence that makes us less recognizable as a corpse. But maybe such argument is yet another way we have of distancing ourselves from the deaths of those we love, like our need to dress them up and make them up to disguise their loss of life's color, as if about to awake and fix us Swedish pancakes, as my grandmother used to do. Viewings and visitations and wakes are less frequent now, and bodies are being cremated rather than being encountered, so we can remember them alive rather than dead. In my view, this does a disservice to our friend Death trying to tell us something. During a period in which I was considering my own cremation without a viewing, a friend who is a Catholic priest told me he wants to see me dead when I die, so he can say goodbye to the friend he loved.

It was not to be cremation for my grandmother. No, this was in the days when the casket was brought to the house, and so she lay there in the living room surrounded by flowers. My mother lifted the thin veil draped over the open casket so each of us children might touch Grandma's hand one last time. "See how soft her skin is," my mother said, which it was, though I didn't really want to touch her, and undoubtedly wanted to wash my hands afterward as if death might be catching. I was too young to appreciate the metaphor of the thin veil between us and death. My grandmother's body was there overnight, though I don't know if there was a round-the-clock vigil as I would later see in the movies, replete with candles and prayers. I do think the coffin lid was closed, tucking Grandma in for the night.

On a much later visit to her grave in the cemetery, my grandfather, her husband, who lived to be ninety-five years of age, said to me with his usual understated wit, "Yes, when you get to be my age, you have to come out here to visit some of your friends." Already his wife and their firstborn infant daughter were buried there, along with my great uncle for whom my Uncle Roy was named. I was named for both, bearing Roy as my middle name. My mother had had the dubious duty as a child to go with her grandmother to her Uncle Roy's grave to assure that my great grandmother would return, given the grief she bore at the death of her son. The family knew she would not do herself in if she had the responsibility of getting little Mildred safely home. Her Uncle Roy's death haunted my mother enough that to the end of her life she would not let us rock a rocking chair without someone in it because that had been done in her own home (bad luck even then) the day they learned of the young Roy's accident working on the railroad, crushed between two trains before the railroad got smart and moved parallel tracks further apart. "Poor little Mildred will have no more Uncle Roy," he had said to her on his deathbed.

I don't remember my grandmother's funeral service, but I do think of so many funeral services for grandparents and other relatives in which the ministers did not seem to know the departed very well, even sometimes saying they didn't know them at all, which in my view, was always too much information. The minister is to lead us in our grief, not his (and it was "his" in those days), as well as in our thanksgiving for the life that touched us. My father's parents, for instance, lived on a farm on the Missouri side of the border from Pittsburg, and didn't get to church much, except by radio and later, television. So though they may not have been known to some preening preacher, they were certainly known to us, and more so to God, whom preachers claim to represent. The preacher not knowing them, or not knowing them well, always seemed to imply a deficit in the deceased, as if they apparently hadn't been to church much, thereby excusing the pastor for his ignorance and occasional laziness, providing, as he sometimes did, a conveyor belt funeral.

Death gives us permission to do things that are, in a sense, countercultural. One of two times that I saw my father break down and cry, countering the cultural notion that men don't cry, was in front of his own father's casket. The other time would be when he offered grace over what would be our final meal together as a family before his own death, when he extended the thanksgivings to include his "wonderful family." And I had witnessed firsthand the very great disappointment on his face when we drove from California, and went straight to his dying mother's hospital room, only to find it empty and being made up for the next patient. She had died earlier in the afternoon in the presence of my brother and Aunt Helen and other relatives. My mother, probably feeling responsible herself that my father had missed the last bit of his mother's life, said something like: if only we had hurried a little more that morning and had not stopped along the way, we might have arrived before she died. The effect of this was to make me feel very guilty, because I had a childhood tendency to dawdle getting ready in the morning, and had insisted we stop at a drive-through for ice cream earlier that afternoon. While some might write off the insistence to being spoiled, I think it rather grew from a place of anger and resentment deep within that we never had what I considered a "normal" vacation. My dad's three weeks of vacation were spent either at home doing jobs around the house or making the long trek to the Midwest to visit relatives. Thus my guilt was deepened exponentially.

I envied my brother his experience, being there at the moment of my grandmother's death, having driven in his Volkswagen bug "straight through" to Kansas without stopping. Later, when he worked during college delivering dinners for a chain called Chicken Delite, he came home to change his soaked clothes after pulling a woman who had drowned from the pool of an apartment building to which he had been making a delivery. Again, I envied his proximity to death. The latter experience seemed to make him, in the moment, pensive, reflective, and sad. But the earlier experience he had seemed to dismiss with his discomfort at our Aunt Helen's dramatic reaction, sobbing loudly, "Mama's gone!" and hugging everyone in the room.

Why did I want to be there at the moment of death—preferably someone else's, of course? Partly I imagined it to be a moment of revelation, an epiphany, a look into what lay beyond, even a sacred moment. Too, it was the dangerous thrill of standing on the edge of an abyss, witnessing, in my innocent mind, the worst that I could imagine, little knowing that death may serve as the ultimate healing for burdens and sufferings far worse than death. Finally, I believe my desire grew from an intuitive notion that life is not full or complete without death. As a child, I could not have articulated this as I do now, but I remember the sources of my fascination, a fascination that was not unduly or uniquely or morbidly felt alone by me; the fascination that makes most all of us unable to look away as we pass an accident on the road or watch a deathbed scene on film.

Many years later a friend would report the death of one of his best friends to AIDS. Disappointed, he said nothing "spiritual" happened. No great insight or deep emotion passed his friend's lips, who was in a deep sleep if not a coma. There was no fluttering of the curtains at the window; no light arose from the body toward the heavens. Just his friend breathing his last. I chided him a little, saying, "Death isn't 'Hollywood,' with a symphonic orchestra swelling in the background. What was spiritual was you and his other friends gathered around to be there for him in his final moments." But my friend had been looking for what we all hope for in the face of death, a sign of hope, of meaning, of something more, of something beyond. A glimpse of the eternal, *please!* No doubt this comes from the "supernaturalizing" of death, rather than receiving it as a natural part of life. We want the same option for death that we have for fast food: we want it "super-sized."

Some readers will think it morbid that as a child I wanted to be an undertaker, partly because I liked to dig holes in the yard. Once, to my father's dismay, I tried to dig a hole to China, whose streets I thought were just beneath our suburban Los Angeles yard and street—taking the metaphor literally about China's streets being under our own, being on the opposite side of the globe. Taking metaphors literally was the same mistake we made as fundamentalists. The other part of my desire to be an undertaker was because I enjoyed the solemn ritual of finding the right satin-lined jewelry box (watch boxes that snapped shut were ideal tiny coffins) or a shiny tin container for a family parakeet or goldfish or hamster that had passed, preparing its final resting place, covering it with earth and prayer and flowers, and often, some kind of marker. I once dug up a buried parakeet, curious to see what it looked like after a year or so. Such a vocational desire may seem a little macabre, yes, but no more macabre, in my view, than my subsequent childish desire to go into politics.

As if to keep me from feeling immune to its powers because of my young age, Death took a friend in the second grade when I was in the first. His mom and my mom were colleagues in a Christian school in which they both taught first grade. His mom was my first-grade school teacher. Her son Ronnie's heart was too big. Metaphorically, this would have been a wonderful remedy for the world's problems. In reality, however, it could be fatal. Ronnie's adult-sized heart was too large for a child's body, meaning he couldn't play like other children and frequently missed school. The then experimental open-heart surgery promised hope for his condition. The whole school prayed for Ronnie. The night before the surgery, Ronnie's mom told mine that she had cried herself to sleep. Ronnie himself had spent his last evening on earth showing another kid in the pediatric ward that an oxygen tent was nothing to be afraid of, a kindly heroic story the adults would later tell to comfort themselves. Even now I'm hesitant to say Ronnie's story proved the lame joke about the operation being a success, but the patient died. Hesitant, because I have an appropriate reverence and love for Ronnie, as well as his destiny. But that was the case. Ronnie survived the operation, which gave our school great hope, but his little body gave out in the recovery room. My mother and I learned it when we got home from school that day. She went immediately to her room to cry. I went to the room I shared with my brother and the two rock n' roll songs that played on his radio in those moments became forever associated with Ronnie's death for me. Funny how that happens.

As I had for my grandmother, I went to the funeral, and saw Ronnie lying there in his little casket, the same white gauze-like material draped loosely from its open lid, giving him a heavenly, apparitional, even dreamy appearance. I felt guilty. I had been to his last birthday party, bringing him a gift, and yet forgetting to tie onto its ribbon a toy harmonica that I had intended to include. I kept meaning to give it to him. Now it was too late. Writing this now, I understand what a very small, even trivial thing this was. But for years that little gift decoration served as a heavy burden. I doubted myself. Had I held it back because I wanted it? Or was it just procrastination on my part? Either way, I experienced it as a grave sin. And to whom could I confess? Death gave me a lesson then that would be repeated, over and over: whatever we have to give, must be given now, before it's too late.

I would think the fundamentalist Christians who inhabited my school struggled with their prayers for Ronnie not being answered. I would think my mom struggled herself with a God who would not save an innocent child's life. I was not apprised of this; nor do I remember considering it myself at the time. God's will was something else we believed in, fell back on, when prayers were not answered. Jesus, himself an innocent, would pray in the garden of Gethsemane, "Not my will, but thine, be done." The specter of a father's will requiring the death of his son did not strike me with the same horror it does today. But it surely set up the acceptability of the death of other innocents in the minds and hearts of these Christians who believed Christ's bloody death somehow atoned for their sins. I don't know if this paragraph will make it into my final manuscript; it seems so speculative about what I may have thought, and what others may have thought then. Adding that sentence, however, makes this paragraph more honest.

I do remember an elderly lady passing Ronnie's open casket with the comment, "It should have been me, not you." I puzzled over this observation. Could one make a deal like that, my life for his? When my sister safely made a trek to the headquarters of Youth for Christ in Indiana for a Bible drill team competition at the same time my paternal grandfather died, the absurd conclusion offered by relatives, maybe even by my mom, was he would have volunteered his own life to ensure her safety. "Did God work that way?" I wondered in all childish innocence.

My memories and my chronology as a child are hazy in my mind, but now, as I look back, I cannot help but wonder if these early experiences of death did not influence my desire to go forward at an altar call and accept Jesus as "my personal Savior." It was neither an impetuous nor impulsive act elicited by the emotions of the moment, which often rode high upon the conclusion of a Baptist sermon and final hymn with its altar call and inevitable multiple verses. I had discussed "going forward" (as we called it) with my parents beforehand. Probably my careful planning was an early hint that I was predestined to be Presbyterian, who resist not only emotion but spontaneity as well. I don't think I was motivated by fear of my own death, which I hardly thought possible at the time. My child's idea of what I was doing was that I was somehow permanently joining myself to my family and Jesus and God forever. I never wanted to be without them. I wanted to belong. I wanted to be with those I loved and those who loved me in life and in death.

The whole family together forever.

Mrs. Witter was our piano teacher. My sister and brother fared better than I did under her tutelage, actually learning to play well. She served as a role model for me as well—but not her musicianship: her printed instructions. I so admired her penmanship; that should have been a clue as to my real aspirations: writing, not music. Mr. Witter tuned our piano, though his "real" work was some kind of business. The whole family was musical; the son and daughter were gifted students of music and casual friends of my brother and sister.

It was, as I remember, a Saturday morning. Saturday was a mixed blessing growing up. No school, but I loved school, or at least I loved the structure it gave my day. My dad worked on Saturday, unfortunately. My mom would get up very early to fix his breakfast before work, then return to bed for a little while. Many Saturday mornings I remember her shouting at me to wake up and put the trash barrels out—something I should have done the night before—because the trash men were coming down the street. Panic would seize me that I wouldn't get them out in time, and I would be faced with their unemptied recrimination throughout the coming week, a feeling of failure at accomplishing one of my few household chores.

But I also remember bouncing with my brother and sister and mom on her bed Saturday mornings, before or after breakfast, and we would sit and visit and enjoy a little time together with nothing to do but laugh and talk and dream. A whole empty day stretched out before us, a day of housecleaning and laundry and reading books (never magazines: early it was instilled in me by my mother that if I had time to read, I should be reading a book) and watching television. My sister and years later, my brother, would drive Mom to the store to do the weekly grocery shopping, if my father had not done so the night before. (Strangely, as earlier mentioned, my mother never learned to drive.) And I would be left alone, a time I also loved, but also a lonely time when I wished my friends from school were closer. Going to a parochial school meant fellow students were dispersed throughout my then-known universe, the 500 square miles of Los Angeles.

Mom sometimes left me lamb chops to broil for my lunch; she knew how I loved them, but she never fixed them for dinner because Dad did not. I might watch a little TV Saturday afternoon, and I remember seeing a lot of winter sports—skiing, slalom, ski-jumping, etc. Though I did not like sports generally, I enjoyed the spectacle and the snow-covered mountains and the announcer's friendly voice, and I felt connected to a world ("The Wide World of Sports") far beyond my own. There were also old movies that played on TV, such as *The Boy with Green Hair*, with whom I identified. In the film, which was made two years before I was, the boy's hair had mysteriously turned green (mine by contrast was bright red and curly), and he was taunted for being different (as was I), and finally conformed, having it shaved off. (I, meanwhile, dreamed of having what I was certain was the ideal: straight, blonde hair.) But something changed his mind. A priest? A relative? Someone persuaded him that there was nothing wrong with his difference, and the movie ended (as I remember) with his determination to let his hair grow back, even if it turned out green. I did not know then that the movie was made as Hollywood's response to the Red Scare and the required conformity of the McCarthy period.

Parallel in theme was the French film, *The Red Balloon*, which my mother took a shine to, borrowing a copy periodically from the Burbank library and showing it to successive classes of first graders. My mother was, I believe, the first teacher at that Christian school to learn how to thread a movie projector and to use a tape recorder as educational tools! And she was one of the few who resisted with her sense of humor, benign mischief, and greater openness to the world that school's conformist, fundamentalist approach to life. Fundamentalism, I came to see, was death in another form, and these particular fundamentalists looked upon movies with suspicion. *The Red Balloon* was about a boy followed by a red balloon, and like the boy with green hair, he was taunted by his classmates because of it. The balloon followed him to school, where it was forced to stay outside, and home, where his mother cast it out. It was unwelcome at church as well. But, each time, it just waited until the little boy reappeared. Other little boys decide to take it away, but the movie is saved from a sad ending by a rebellion of all the balloons held down by their captors.

I had green hair in several ways; and many red balloons dogged me. My time alone on Saturdays gave me an opportunity to understand this. Eventually death would teach me to accept my green hair and my red balloon before it was too late. Death would teach me to accept who I was and welcome that which would help me fly.

All these colors were lost on our black and white television. Unlike my peers, we would not have color television until my dad's first bout with cancer when my older brother and sister bought him one while I was in college. The possibility of his death had brought color into our living room! Funny how watching everything in black and white had "colored" my view of the world! For the longest time, I always thought cars should either be black or white. In fact, I've only once owned a colored car, and that was by happenstance. My first was black, my second white, and the present one is grey! Our family television paralleled the moral sensibilities of our religion, seeing everything in black and white. The fact that we endured long periods when the television didn't work and my dad didn't want to pay to have it repaired paralleled the frequent failure of our moral outlook. The family joke was that we would tune our broken TV into Oral Roberts and lay hands on it as the evangelist squealed "H-e-a-l!" Sound we had, the picture we didn't. Just because we were fundamentalists didn't mean we had no sense of humor. And televangelists were "over the top" even for us.

Saturday afternoons stretched out to Saturday nights, when we ate the pork roast with beans or Irish stew or pot roast or Mexican chili that had been pop-pop-popping in the stovetop pressure cooker all afternoon, wafting aromas that made one sick with hunger or, in the case of pork roast and beans, which I didn't like, just plain sick. Saturday night I'd have my bath for church Sunday morning, and, smelling clean and fresh in my laundered pajamas, I'd stay up to watch *The Fabulous 52!*, which broadcasted a different movie each week at 11:15 p.m. on the CBS affiliate in Los Angeles. Mom would usually fall asleep during the movie, but Dad and I would stay awake and finish it. One of those movies was Frank Capra's *Lost Horizon*. In a gentle blending of East and West, this movie depicted a mythical Himalayan village in which want and crime were unknown, life was lived well and long, and spirituality was central but practiced in moderation, The movie captured my young imagination.

Anyway, as I started to say before a digression I hope my editor will leave in the final manuscript, Saturday was my longest day, a day whose structure I had more freedom to shape than any other day of the week, making me feel sorry for those children today whose free time is overly scheduled by ambitious or well-intentioned parents. Small wonder that my life now consists of a succession of "Saturdays," having chosen to be a writer. It is a life blessed by more freedom than the lives of others, though it is also fraught with fear, having no imposed structure but my own, and having no assured income, especially when writing something like this book, entirely on speculation. Yet it does stretch my days, it does stretch my life. And it offers me sanctuary to "stand under" (as Camus wrote of it), if not to wholly understand, life. If my sexuality as well as my spirituality serve as my "green hair," writing is my "red balloon."

Against the backdrop normality of these typical Saturdays, one Saturday proved very different from all others. My sister's radio reported a plane bound for Venezuela out of New York had exploded "in a ball of flame." We knew that the Witter children had gone to visit their uncle who worked in the Venezuelan oil fields, a promise their parents kept when both had reached at least sixteen years of age. My mother was always making possible personal connections out of names or events on the news. If, for example, a Joe Bowerman were on the news, she'd wonder if it was the Joe Bowerman she'd grown up with, or even farther-fetched, if he was related to the Bowerman family which lived in Pittsburg, Kansas. This time, when she wondered aloud if this was their plane, a phone call confirmed that she was right.

We went to the Witter house to find Mrs. Witter, still in her bathrobe, being comforted by a few friends and neighbors. I can only imagine the mother's grief, my imagination a pale bloodless apparition next to the real thing of losing a child, let alone two, let alone one's only children, and in a horrific midair explosion. My own childlike incomprehension instead regarded their deaths with wonder: to die in a spectacular plane crash ("a ball of flame") and have it reported through the media! One of the few items found in the debris floating in the waters off the New York City skyline was a music satchel that belonged to one of them, filled with sheet music that belonged to the other. A newspaper picked up the human interest angle of the story, about how this musically-gifted and accomplished brother and sister shared their music and their love of music. Their bodies were never recovered to my knowledge, and we attended a memorial service for them in their Methodist church. Their parents gave my brother and sister and me some of their personal effects, which included a wooden bowl I still have.

A year or so later, we would attend the funeral of their father in the same church. Mrs. Witter had called him in for dinner. When he didn't come, she found him dead from a heart attack in his garage workshop. Not surprisingly, Mrs. Witter never recovered from all of this. Friends said she lived on cigarettes and coffee and flew frequently; possibly, as my mother conjectured, hoping her plane too would crash and end her sad life. When I was in high school, a neighbor happened to see her name in an obituary column. She had moved to the Northwest, returned to her childhood Catholicism, developed cancer, and now had been returned for a viewing and a burial alongside her husband and at least the gravestone names of her dearly beloved children. We saw her one last time, now a small, frail body, wasted away by grief and cancer, hands clutching a rosary as if a lifeline to her family. We arrived just before they closed the coffin, and we joined the small procession of neighbors and friends to a garden in Forest Lawn.

I was so moved that I began work on a forty-stanza poem about the whole family (shades of Emmeline Grangerford!?); eventually cut to seventeen stanzas, and then filed away altogether, just as their lives had been cut short, and hidden by the fates. What I remember from the poem is the metaphor of "piano strings slashed by airplane wing." I could not master death, but I discovered I could ferret out from under its pall meaning, even beauty, through writing. Writing became a means of asserting control over something over which I have little and ultimately no control; feeling empowered in the midst of vulnerability. Envisioning a meaning in death or despite death overcomes the impotence death would like to impose on life. Jean Paul Sartre's fictional victim of castration nonetheless asserts his power by looking his perpetrators in the eye. There's a difference between being a collaborator with death (i.e. Emmeline Grangerford, perhaps even the hospice worker described earlier), and joining the Resistance ("Do not go gently into that good night," as the poet Dylan Thomas urged his father.).

In contrast to the brief and fixed lives of the Witters, my family members' lives have had the quality and quantity of a Saturday, my longest day as a child, stretching out before us, ready to be structured in our freedom, ready to be filled with so many happy memories, creative moments, and difficult challenges. Theirs was such an unusual case, all dying within so few years of one another, that their lives are almost bracketed in my heart and mind as an exception to God's will or the way things are supposed to be. Were their lives rewarding and full, even so? If the answer to that question depends on whether they loved each other well, it seemed as though they did.

What a maudlin story, you might say. It's hard to tell the story without becoming maudlin. I apologize. I was so very young when all of this happened, so full of emotion and passion, that the story has left a permanently nostalgic mark on me. In addition to my need to write of it, death taught me its arbitrariness: one family taken, the other family spared. I started just now to write "and death's lack of compassion," and then it occurred to me, that having the worst grief any parent could bear, the taking of the father's and mother's lives early saved them years of pain and regret over their children's deaths. Death whispers there is some grief whose healing only comes when we let go of life entirely.

Chapter Two

Death in Public

T hose growing up these days with the terrorist threat and anxiety over weapons of mass destruction might have an inkling of what it was like to grow up during the early days of the Cold War, when nuclear annihilation of the planet hung over us like Damocles' sword, or closer to reality, like the radioactive clouds that passed over parts of the planet after a nuclear test. But only an inkling. For the comparatively petty little grip that terrorists hold on our world today is but a fraction of the grip that any leader of the U.S.S.R. or the U.S. had over the entire human civilization—no, the entire creation—in those times. Osama bin Laden and all his violent, puny-hearted brethren could never amass what one person could accomplish (or rather, destroy) with the push of a button. The emphasis today on security and preparedness, from everything from bottled water to duct tape, is extremely reminiscent of the bomb shelters that people built then, as if salvation were possible in a nuclear holocaust. Viewing schoolchildren's "duck and cover" practice on the evening news after 9/11 parallels the "duck and cover" routines of the Cold War in which we were drilled, as if school desks could ever inhibit the havoc wreaked by a nuclear or now, biological, weapon. A part of me suspects that these exercises are intended to frighten us rather than protect us; manipulating in us a paranoia that excuses a "first strike" mentality, whether on a designated opponent or our own civil rights.

During seventh grade in junior high, at my Christian school in southern California, we were holding a school-wide assembly when Louise Gerald, our principal, came in and triumphantly announced in her Southern accent that the Soviet freighters had turned around, respecting President Kennedy's naval blockade during the October 1962 Cuban missile crisis. We cheered, and then we prayed our gratitude to God that we had been spared, for we all had imagined our lives on the brink. I wonder when some smart and greedy lawyer will finally realize the money to be made demanding compensation for all the children who endured this constant stress at the hands of the Soviet and U.S.governments. We at least deserve our share of talk-show air time! The Free World was a misnomer or at least an inaccuracy, because we were never entirely free as long as half the world was hostage to dictators, poverty, hunger, ignorance, and the anger and hatred and jealousy and envy they breed—any of which could have had catastrophic nuclear consequences.

The first story I remember writing from my imagination described my witnessing a mushroom cloud rise on the horizon outside the living room windows of our home in a suburb of Los Angeles. The story expressed a sense of dread and doom, intimations of our worst fears. The mushroom cloud on the horizon outside reflected the death that haunted our interior horizons. Yet, perversely, there was also a fascination with such utter destruction, echoing the psychological tenet that what we most fear frequently attracts us. (This could account as well for writing or reading this book!) Previous generations grew up with perhaps far more violence and plague and wars manifest in their communities and countries, but we had the unprecedented "opportunity" to witness yet more on television and in the movies. We were not the first generation *to imagine* that the world could be ended by a great disaster, such as a flood or a plague or a war. But we were the first generation *to know* that the world could be ended by a simple mistake. And we were the first generation to grow up with the awareness that "modern" civilization could kill six million Jews, and millions more dissidents, homosexuals, Roma, religious minorities, and other "queers." We grew up, though, not knowing any better, like many a child who is the victim of abuse. Our nuclear mindset served as an invisible backdrop to how we lived our lives. We lived normal lives in a culture always on the precipice of death. No doubt that's why, when I witnessed Soviet Premier Khrushchev waving from his motorcade as he drove through my neighborhood during his visit to Los Angeles in September 1959, the crowds did not wave or cheer or boo, but stood in frozen silence.

When I was in second grade, we were told that a classmate's mother had been killed in a car accident. To be "killed," in my young mind, was more exotic than simply dying. It was "untimely," garnered greater sympathy, added drama, and thus was more likely to gain the attention of the media, our only certain omnipresent god. I imagined the headline in the next day's newspaper, "PEGGY'S MOM KILLED IN CAR CRASH." There was some glamour in it, even martyrdom when accompanied by religious overtones. My sister was active in Youth for Christ, and I remember monthly YFC rallies in the Church of the Open Door in downtown Los Angeles—with a neon cross on its church tower flashing "JESUS SAVES." The rallies went late into Saturday night when I would have preferred being home in bed, but instead I would be rudely awakened by the brass ensemble after the sermon that had lulled me to sleep with its rhythmic, undulating preacher-phrasing and its unintelligible adult talk. One service was devoted to two teenagers, a boy and girl couple, who had been killed in a freeway accident returning from Disneyland. They were made out to be Christian martyrs because it had been a church outing, and they were very active in the music programs of their church and in YFC. Feelings ran high, and I thought it would be nice to die a martyr, though even then, a mere child, I wondered how these adult leaders could portray this unfortunate teen accident as some kind of martyrdom. I knew little of the manipulation of evangelists, who mercilessly used teenage deaths to corral unsuspecting youths to conversion. Later, an evangelist visiting our church emotionally told the story of teens he supervised who slept in a car on a snowy mountain and died of carbon monoxide from the car heater. In my view, victims of his inadequate supervision were being used to cash in salvation chips as enough young people came forward during the altar call to fill an entire front pew, moved as they were toward conversion or "re-dedication" by early deaths that could have been their own. The trump card for one visiting evangelist in our church was when he announced during the Sunday sermon that Marilyn Monroe had been found earlier that morning, a victim of suicide. I felt a shock wave go over the previously unaware congregation, and of course she was used as an example of why we needed Jesus as our Lord and Savior in this troubling world. Poor Marilyn, a pawn even in death. If only she had gotten to Billy Graham that time she tried to reach out to him.

But being killed, or killed as a martyr, was trumped by being assassinated. President John F. Kennedy was assassinated, which meant being killed as a kind of martyr and as an especially great man. That, I thought, would be the finest death. To be great, to be killed, to be considered a martyr! This trinitarian formula for being immortalized would be the best of all. Yet, if asked if I could alter one event in history, this would be the one I would choose. To this day I cannot watch the Magruder film clip of Kennedy's assassination, or read or hear anything about his death, without my eyes welling with tears and my heart feeling like it could burst with sorrow. Was it my thirteen-year-old innocence that was shattered that November 22, 1963? Was it the idyllic dream of Camelot, that "fleeting wisp of glory," that was forever taken from me?

I was sitting in an English class that Friday when Chuck Brown, a fellow eighth-grader whom I considered the masculine ideal and on whom I had the biggest crush, came in from another classroom and breathlessly tried to tell us what he had heard Principal Louise Gerald telling another class. Chuck was so excited, he was unintelligible, and what I "heard" was that some man from Texas had been shot and was dying on our campus. Some of us nervously laughed in our incomprehension at Chuck's hysteria; later I would fear my laughter might be attributed to my support of Barry Goldwater for president. Our school did not have a P.A. system, so Mrs. Gerald was going from classroom to classroom and finally arrived in ours to deliver the tragic news that President Kennedy had been shot during a visit to Texas. Later, my algebra teacher, Mr. Parrish, would say that it would be unlikely that we would ever experience such a historic event again in our lifetimes. Little did he know; but he was accurate in the sense that this, as I said, would be one historical event I would want to undo. I believe our nation would have been better if President Kennedy had lived to serve two terms; but then, one could never know, and my desire to see the event undone may have less to do with what might have been as it has to do with undoing an event that traumatized the nation and, in particular, me, affecting both national and personal psyches for decades.

Another memory comes to me as I rewrite this portion of the book. One of the teachers with whom my mom exchanged jokes, practical and otherwise, suggested we all go out to dinner together the weekend of Kennedy's assassination. I was privately horrified, as well as certain I would miss something, like maybe an attempt on the new President Lyndon Johnson's life. We *all* thought "conspiracy" in those early days. Going out for dinner Saturday night seemed disrespectful, but my mother's friend thought it would be good for all of us to get away from the media bombardment for an evening. My recollection seems strange because of my surprise at finding the Mexican restaurant packed and festive, the food extraordinarily tasty, even after the death of a president! It was reminiscent of the food people always brought to the home after a family funeral and the ensuing potluck. How good it was to be with people, how good the food! Laughter and frivolity were within reach of tears and sorrow.

Kennedy's death reinforced in metaphorical steel and concrete the phenomenon I experienced in lesser ways and in more modest lives and deaths: Death transformed an individual from an oft-neglected to a highly-regarded person. Mark Twain told us as much in *The Adventures of Tom Sawyer*, in which Tom and Huck had the good fortune of attending their own funerals *alive*, a fantasy I and, no doubt, almost everyone has had at one time or another. Tom and Huck were deeply moved by how dearly they were loved, and thus surprised at the angry recrimination they encountered upon their "resurrection."

I've long thought it a shame that we save our eulogies of others' lives for their deaths. "Eulogy" comes from Greek words meaning "good words," and wouldn't it be better to offer good words to people while they're living? As a child, I identified with youthful protagonists in Disney-style programs and films who were misunderstood or unappreciated by their families until their lives were in danger. "They'll be sorry when I'm gone!" I would comfort myself. A poem about an adolescent's death, that I wrote in my own adolescence, included the refrain "'he would've wanted it this way'—it's easier to say what he would've wanted now he's passed away." My poetic stanza was a reflection on parents trying to give their child in death what they had failed to give in life. From adolescence into early adulthood, I found myself being conscious of things I did that might be remembered at my funeral, collecting achievements as a kind of death résumé that would then be listed and lauded. I have to wonder at my hunger for affirmation: did it originate in the fear common to most of us, that if people really knew us, they wouldn't like us? I don't believe that mine was a neurotic fear. I believed I held a secret that could negate in other's eyes all the good I had done, even if I were to save the world!

Death seemed a faster and easier way to sainthood than sanctification. The Rodney Dangerfields of the world finally get their respect. Indeed, we call our homages to the dead "paying our respects." Allan was the "Rodney Dangerfield" of our high school. He was a little odd and the butt of jokes, even from my fellow Christian schoolmates, though by that time I was in public, not parochial, school. As was my wont, I felt sorry for him and tried to be friendly. I always gravitated to the "runt" of the litter, because I felt myself to be one too, the consummate if closeted outsider. Allan's locker was close to mine, and one Friday he showed me a "prize" catch, a ball of wax he thrust in my face, gleefully announcing, "This is genuine mortician's wax." Appalled, I stepped back, as if one could "catch" death by touching or smelling one of its accoutrements. (Or, as many of our mothers said, "You don't know where it's been!") As we walked to the music room where we both had choir, he explained (rather chillingly, given his obvious pleasure) how he had obtained the wax on a visit to a mortuary, and proceeded to tell me in gruesome detail how the bodies are prepared, veins slashed so the blood flows into drains on the floor, in preparation for being infused with embalming fluid. It was Halloween weekend, and, as I recall, he had actually witnessed this firsthand, or at least, a mortician who had witnessed this firsthand had supplied him with the gory details. He was going to use the wax for his Halloween costume. When we arrived, to my great relief, at the choir room, my friends Margie and Judi observed to Allan that his face was crimson red. "That's because Chris walks so fast," Allan said in mock complaint, and I felt guilty, because I hadn't thought of his heart problem, part of the reason he got taunted growing up. I may have walked a little faster to bring an early end to his grisly description, but also, being such a good little boy, I didn't want to be late for my favorite class.

The following Monday, Allan was absent from choir. As we wondered where he was, Margie joked that maybe he'd been spirited away with the other goblins on Halloween, and we laughed, though I did so guiltily, because I felt I was somehow being unfaithful to Allan. Just then our choir director and teacher Mr. George Attarian came in. He must've overheard, because he rather brusquely announced (out of character for him) that he wasn't going to take any guff today, and then explained that Allan had died over the weekend. His heart condition had made him vulnerable to a simple virus. I flashed back to his crimson face caused by my walking pace, and had a sinking feeling. Had I inadvertently contributed to his death? Then I had a sickening feeling as I realized that now his body was undergoing the same mortician's assault he had described to me just three days before. A few of us gathered in a counselor's office to speak in somber tones about his passing. In death, this "Rodney Dangerfield" received new respect.

The reader might consider this book to be my own "mortician's ball of wax" and that I have a preoccupation with death that parallels poor Allan's. It would only heighten your suspicions if I were to dismiss such a perspective out of hand. I know we're not supposed to speak of ethnic distinctions—as if they were all stereotypically inaccurate—but the Irish in me resonated with an article I read years ago asserting that the Irish love to ruminate on lost love, death, and regrets; this indeed may be why I write this book. But I've written fourteen books and published twelve that have more to do with life than death; and I would hope this book too would point toward life. Death forces us back on life, as a shut door forces us to find another passageway, a roadblock prompts us to take a detour, or a great loss encourages us to savor what remains. Death is a natural, final guide, as opposed to a supernatural God or belief system. Unlike the latter, we have certain knowledge of it, though we live largely in denial. Death delivers an ultimatum, while faith insists that whatever death can do, it's not over till it's over—a ubiquitous Yogi Berra truism—that is perhaps just another form of denial. Death is a moment we will each certainly face (though many of us who were Christian wished Jesus would return before that moment, or that perhaps we could be "translated" as Enoch or "taken" as Moses, rather than endure the pain of death). Eternity is a matter of faith, but so is time itself. What we have is the moment, and we're not even certain how long our moment is. Indian poet and philosopher Rabindranath Tagore assured, "The butterfly has but moments, and yet has time enough." It is because I believe we have "time enough" that Death can be taken as a friendly coach for life.

Eventually I noted that in death, a certain respectful mythology can arise around even a bad person, such as, "He must've suffered to become so angry. . . or bitter . . . or hateful." In my forties, living in Atlanta, I met an out-of-town friend for a drink one evening, yet didn't invite her home for dinner because I did not want to confess my desire to watch the televised memorial service that evening for former President Nixon, to whom we had both been diametrically opposed politically and whose paranoid manipulations cast a pall on the presidency in both of our minds. I was embarrassed that, in death, I felt a kinship with one whose policies I had protested in demonstrations, letters, and opinion pieces. The solemn ceremony dignified him in a way he did not always dignify himself. And there was a grudging respect to be paid for his accomplishments despite his sins. In the final months of his battle with cancer, Hubert Humphrey is said to have phoned his Congressional colleagues "on both sides of the aisle" because facing the common denominator made earlier political divisions and disagreements seem far less important than their personal connections. Death writes its own *Book of Virtues.*

A friend of mine holds in contempt any eulogist who includes character flaws of the deceased, even in a good-humored way. Part of his attitude no doubt stems from being raised in the South, where people may be polite to the point of duplicity, if not dishonesty. But my friend's attitude (one of the reasons I've invited him to be my eulogist!) reveals a regard we hold for the dead that we don't always have for the living. "To speak ill of the dead," is bad form, probably because death transmutes an individual to the eternal, invisible, and sacred realm. When John F. Kennedy died, his enemies spoke of him as noble, his detractors described him as friend, and his supporters elevated him to sainthood. (Thus I was horrified by an exception: a relative who supported Goldwater quipped, "Thanksgiving came early for the Goldwaters this year." This would be my initiation into the genre of dark or gallows humor which follows all national tragedies, a way for pundits to cheat death of its power to silence and intimidate as well as immortalize.)

Kennedy became a cultural icon. His brother Bobby would follow him into that pantheon, as would the Reverend Martin Luther King Jr., whose devoted life as well as death in pursuit of long-denied civil rights for African Americans made him a true martyr, not simply an imagined one. Appropriate white guilt and an emerging black pride made King's birthday a holiday (a "holy day"). King and Bobby Kennedy died just five years after President Kennedy, and together, the three embodied the optimism of an era. Thus there was a collective sense of cultural loss that, along with Vietnam and Watergate, heightened cynicism within the United States and in me.

Of course not all sense of cultural loss is political. I was very much surprised when a member of a church I served was devastated by the death of a very different kind of king, Elvis Presley. I appreciated him and his music and felt his early death sad; but for my friend, his death meant much more. I would not understand until John Lennon was shot and killed. Younger generations would not understand how either death could profoundly affect someone until the untimely deaths of Kurt Cobain, Aaliyah, or Michael Jackson touched their hearts. The deaths of cultural icons affect us in a very different way from other deaths, and vary from person to person in their effect. As a child, I thought the world would end if my hero, Walt Disney, died. The one time I saw him, just a few feet away, showing a dignitary around Disneyland, I remember looking up at him in awe, as if I were seeing God. All of us can think of others in the public eye whose deaths touched us profoundly—performers, artists, writers, philosophers, theologians, politicians, actors, and so on. The death of a cultural icon goes beyond the feeling that we have lost a "friend," someone known to us. The death of a cultural icon punctuates the ending of an era of our lives, diminishes our culture and thus our experience of the world, and reminds us that none of us—no matter how accomplished—get out of this life alive. Everyone will die, but we think of extraordinary people as invincible in a way we do not think of ordinary people. "No man is an island," John Donne truthfully wrote, "send not to know for whom the bell tolls; it tolls for thee." In each public death knell our cultural as well as personal finitude reverberates.

Yet at the same time that the death of a cultural icon takes away, it enhances the culture through myth. Think of Marilyn Monroe and James Dean as but two examples. Sometimes the icon transcends death bodily in the cultural consciousness, ranging from Jesus' resurrection appearances to posthumous visits from recognized saints, all the way to Elvis "sightings."

Public death seemed easier to take than private death, whether as an icon, a martyr, or simply a victim—perhaps because it is a death shared by the whole society. A friend infected by HIV told me that he could handle death better if it occurred within a grand and unique gesture, such as Monroe's dramatic suicide or Dean's spectacular car crash, but to be part of a collective death such as AIDS was too anonymous to be satisfying. ("Satisfying" is a strange term to be used in this context, given that it implies being "full," and one death may seem as full or as empty as another. Yet, like real estate, location, or in this case context, is everything, even in death.)

As a child I once feared dying not only an anonymous death, but a stupid one as well. For some reason, I had taken to sucking on stones. Their mineral taste was pleasing to me. But on a swing, leaning back while laughing at a playmate's antics, I swallowed one, casting me into a depth of despair. I was sure I would die. I couldn't tell anyone of my fear because I couldn't confess my strange secret pleasure. My mother interpreted it as my just being excited about my upcoming birthday, when in reality I was depressed about my (assumed) upcoming death day! Again, that weekend, I went to one of my sister's Youth for Christ gatherings (they seemed always associated with death), this time in a small Hollywood chapel, and I remember looking out to the sky above the partly opened stained glass window beside my pew thinking of my funeral in a church such as this.

I had heard about the therapeutic qualities of prunes, and asked my mother about them. Finally I admitted to her what had happened, and our family doctor, who took such things in stride, said I probably had or would pass it. But it was the first time I seriously thought I might die.

Worse than an anonymous death would be an ignominious death. Sunday morning after President Kennedy's assassination I opted to stay home from church and slept in. When I awoke, I turned on the TV, fixed myself a bowl of cereal, sat down in front of the television, and watched Lee Harvey Oswald being brought out and then shot. It was stunning. Most Americans watching were, I believe, in some sense grateful to Jack Ruby, saved as they were from a long and painful trial, as well as having had their outrage channeled through the barrel of a gun. Of course the shortsightedness of that solution helped give rise to conspiracy theories, which I view as unresolved emotions in the face of enormous tragedy. I believe that unresolved emotions also give rise to divine conspiracy theories, as in, "It must've been God's will." Poor God! We hardly give thanks to God for life, and yet we often blame God for death!

To witness death "live" seems almost a contradiction, but I would experience "live" death on television again when I watched the space shuttle Challenger blow up and the World Trade Center towers collapse. With round-the-clock news coverage and internet media in all parts of the globe, we may anticipate more and more death being covered "live." The coverage of contemporary air wars are a step removed from this, because dropping bombs, unfortunately, does not give us eyewitness knowledge of the demise of their human targets. If they did, even such "neat and tidy" wars might be less tolerable. Peacemakers, ranging from mere accommodators to true visionaries, have the spiritual imagination to "see" so-called "collateral" damage, thus motivating their peacemaking activities. But most of us have the "gift" of denial.

The biggest celebrity to die in my lifetime was God. The "death of God" theology was one of the rare times in recent memory that any thoughtful theology made the covers of the weekly newsmagazines. You see, God is a cosmic Rodney Dangerfield who often only gets respect in death: God's or our own. The media give God little respect and as little attention as possible. Many of God's so-called representatives steal God's spotlight, as well as thunder, by deploying God on scapegoats—those unjustly blamed for everything from weakening societal values and structures to natural disasters—thus making the media and the multitudes cynical about all things God. The death of God, though, was the death of our old ideas of God, the very ideas that fuel those self-styled frontmen for God: bloody atonement theories, damnation and hellfire scenarios, antagonism between religion and science, exclusivistic claims that damn non-believers or other-believers, or belief in a Supreme "Creationist" quite willing to destroy "his" own artwork in the end. But God is bigger than our limited perspectives. Mark Twain could be speaking for God when he said, "Reports of my death have been greatly exaggerated." Though we may conceptualize or experience God in different ways than our ancestors, the "something-beyond-our-comprehension" is very much alive, independent of our understanding or even our simple recognition. Contemporary theologian Marcus Borg invites atheists, "Tell me about the God you don't believe in."

The one thing that I think old-time religion has gotten right is that God somehow has ordained death, though neither as a kind of punishment, nor as a retribution for "original" sin or unoriginal sins. That we could cause God to do anything contrary to God's will in choosing life for us seems absurdly egotistical, if not "egolatrous." One only has to look outside as the seasons change to recognize death as a part of life, the creation renewing itself. Has the fading blossom sinned? Has the bulb some great virtue that it resurrects each spring? Part of our fear of death, I believe, comes from associating it with sin, failure, loss, and punishment, rather than as part of the natural cycle of life.

John Rice, a friend and Methodist minister who himself would die in a bizarre accident at the early age of fifty, told me of asking his father how he was doing after being diagnosed with a fatal illness. "I'm dying," his father shrugged matter-of-factly, as if to say that this too was a part of life that he was going both to endure and to appreciate. As we reach for that level of nonchalance about our own deaths, we may dare to think of death as a friendly reminder to get on with life as long as it lasts.

Early on I adopted the posture that "if this is all there is to life, thanks be to God." I trust God, or the sacred impulse that led to this existence that I have experienced, to do the right thing in the larger scheme of things. If ongoing existence in a spiritual realm is part of that larger scheme, well then, hallelujah. If not, well then, hallelujah. I describe this as "adopting a posture" because I don't always have this much faith or trust. (I find the less I believe, the more faith I must have!) I believe that ultimately our fear of death is a lack of faith and trust in the divine or cosmic process, whether understood as a personal God or as some kind of life force.

In college I discovered a zest for living in Nikos Kazantzakis's novelized account in *Zorba the Greek* of his encounter with the real Zorba. To throw myself willy-nilly into life as he did, to embrace its troubles and joys, seemed the best way to say to God or the universe: "Thank you!" Zorba thought men like him should live a thousand years, probably because few of us relish life so adequately. At the moment of death itself, he rushed to a window for a final look at the mountains, first laughing, then "whinnying like a horse." He died as he had wanted—eyes wide open, standing on his own, in the face of death.

"If this is all there is to life, thanks be to God" is a posture that does not necessarily help me in accepting the deaths of others, for whom I wish an eternal existence, given the seemingly unfulfilled quality of their lives. Yet how can I judge another's fulfillment? To this question, Death presents an inscrutable face.

Chapter Three
Death by Murder

In all my years of education, including seminary, I never imagined I would personally deal with murder. I would say that the first time caught me unawares, though immediately I realize that's partly the nature of murder. I was in a West Hollywood bar called The Blue Parrot—as you might imagine, a tropically-appointed affair, with gaily-colored drinks holding tiny parasol swizzle sticks. I met someone who worked at the Antiques Guild, a high-end furniture store, and asked if he knew a friend who worked there. The person abruptly (maybe not, maybe it only seemed abrupt at the time, given the nature of the news)announced, "He's dead."

"What?" I asked, incredulous. My negative reaction to the way I was told may have been a vestigial remain of ancient times, when messengers with bad news were summarily killed.

"He was murdered last year." To think a body who had touched my own in intimate ways was now rotting in a grave made me shiver with proximity. That I hadn't been informed troubled me too.

"How?" I asked.

I don't recall if this person gave me all the following details. Some were later gleaned from subsequent news stories about the man's mother raising a fuss, believing the Los Angeles Police

Department was not adequately investigating her son's death because he was gay (to no gay person's surprise). He had received a bullet in the head on a street in Hollywood in the middle of the night, and was found the next morning. When I learned this, I must confess I thought, "Now that's spectacular." Police theorized a drug deal gone bad. His mother, methodically calling everyone in her son's phone book, eventually called me, disputing the police theory. "My son was a good boy," she said. I would not have disputed that, especially to a dead friend's mother, though our definitions of good probably differed. Contrary to her belief, I knew he did drugs and the last time I had seen him, he told me he was being kept by another man, who had put him up in a West Hollywood duplex on Fountain Ave. To this day I wonder if this was the one who did him in, but this speculation was not something I was about to offer his mother. Nor was I about to reveal his sugar daddy or drug forays. And, though this knowledge might impugn her belief in her son as a "good boy," he really was a good guy, undeserving of this fate.

The mother was right about one thing: her contempt for the police investigation was well-founded. She was doing what an L.A.P.D. detective should have done long before, phoning her son's personal phone list. I would have told a detective things I would not have told his mother. After hanging up with her, I considered phoning the police. But previous experience with police bureaucracy made me assume that such a call would be a lost cause. Besides, I did not know him well enough in the final year of his life to offer anything definitive.

Murder and Ministry

That's about as close to murder as anyone comes. But it was to move closer and closer. Shortly thereafter I returned from an out-of-town trip to a phone call from a church member who was also a personal friend, Ron Larason. His former roommate, Carter Courtney, had been arrested for the alleged murder of Danny, Carter's one-time lover. I had met Carter briefly in the apartment that Ron and Carter had shared as roommates. Carter was a jovial, balding, and round (as in delightfully fat) character with a flair for the extravagant and the dramatic. The home, as I recall, was very "Hollywood," a set with faux French Provincial decor with a slight Greek classical tinge to it, probably from the Ionic column pedestals ubiquitous in gay homes of the era. The Greek accents were appropriate for the tragedy about to play out, a drama that would have been fodder for a good "B" melodrama if only the characters had been straight and thus, more marketable. I had liked Carter when I met him, but I did not believe him. He had been a stand-up comic and sometime porn actor (difficult for me to imagine, but people's erotic tastes range considerably). Carter was in the flag corps of the Great American Yankee Freedom Band. He had fallen hard for the trumpet player in the band, a handsome olive-skinned Adonis named Danny. Unbelievably to me, given their disparate appearances, they had become lovers, though their intermediary Cupid was drugs, and a specific one whose nickname I can't even remember—whatever injectable was *au courant* in the late 1970's.

Ron had moved out as the relationship between Carter and Danny grew rocky and violent, the straw breaking the camel's back being a hypodermic needle found by Ron stuck in a cushion of the sofa. Though he remained friendly with Carter, Ron's premonition of disaster proved correct. In his phone call to me, Ron asked if I would visit Carter, who at first had been placed in the prison ward of a hospital for treatment after a suicide attempt following "the incident."

Before I could manage the visit, Danny's present lover came to see me in my office at the church. Doug was a good-looking, earnest, wholesome, sincere, young man, in the most naïve and therefore worst and best senses of those terms. He explained to me what had happened. He and Danny had started dating some time before, Danny wanting to break with Carter, and Doug had helped him, he said, get off the drugs that linked them. Danny and he had been living together when Carter invited Danny over one evening. Danny had indicated to Doug that this would be the last time he would see Carter, an unintended prophecy. As it played out in the courtroom drama that later unfolded, Carter had himself offered a rather cryptic prophecy to a neighbor, "Danny's coming home forever," or something to that effect. They shot up their favorite drug "for old time's sake" and Carter allegedly reminded Danny of their mutual suicide pact. A gun, recently purchased by Carter, was produced and, in what Carter would later describe as a struggle for the gun, it discharged in Danny's chest. To end Danny's suffering, Carter would subsequently claim, he applied another bullet to the head. He left (or mailed?) notes for several people, then drove to a bathhouse where he was a regular, took a room and asked not to be disturbed the remainder of the night, privately intending to commit suicide with pills and a bottle of booze. Toward morning, the management became concerned, broke open his door, and called an ambulance without knowing all that had transpired earlier. Meanwhile, Doug had been concerned for Danny, and came looking for him at Carter's apartment. I don't know how he got in, but he walked into the bedroom and found Danny dead in a pool of blood. As Doug told me this, his eyes downcast, I shuddered, instinctively reaching for his hands and placing mine atop his. He did not cry, but I felt he was not so much withholding tears as he had no more tears to offer. He was already wrung dry from the experience.

I was asked to lead Danny's memorial service in the small sanctuary of our church, West Hollywood Presbyterian on Sunset Boulevard, near the well-known Sunset Strip. An ensemble from the Los Angeles Gay Men's Chorus sang "Danny Boy." There was not a dry eye in the house. I led the gathered friends in speaking their feelings. Interestingly, there was as much if not more grief expressed for Carter as there was for Danny. Carter was well-loved; Danny was not so well-loved. I took it that Danny had been somewhat arrogant, proud of his instrument and good looks, and somewhat manipulative and exploitive in his relationships. In contrast, Carter was generous and extravagant with his affections. How drugs and desire had changed things! After the service, a Mafioso-type character with a hand heavy with gold rings and a wrist laden with gold bands and watch secretively pressed a hundred-dollar bill into my hand to thank me for doing the service.

Meanwhile, Carter had been transferred to the Los Angeles County Jail, and had requested Ron to bring him some personal items from the apartment. Understandably, Ron did not want to go to the apartment alone and asked me to go with him. I did, and we discovered the place where we had once dined together in tasteful surroundings now disheveled by drugs and detectives, a dirty tinge of fingerprint dust on walls and furniture. Noting Ron's hesitancy, I offered to enter the bedroom first, where I found a large cache of brown dried blood on the carpet at the foot of the bed. Never again would I believe film or television versions of violent crime scenes. They are too tidy, absent the ash-like residue of fingerprinting on almost everything; and the blood too red and sparse. It seemed that all the blood Danny's body held was in a giant brown scab at my feet. Ron quickly gathered the toothbrush and other toiletries and tennis shoes we had come for, and we went to the jail. If we lingered at all, it was because I was quite taken with both the horror and holiness of the scene. Something profound had happened here, something that needed to be considered, reflected on and absorbed. It was somehow both scary and sacred and, though I did not think of it then, there was a continuity between this bloodletting and that of ancient sacrifices. Both, in my mind, were misguided expressions of human violence that had nothing to do with either immortal love or demands of divinity, yet having eternal, karmic repercussions for all the souls touched by such acts. Both were intended for at-one-ment— the religious with God or the gods, and the "romantic" between Carter and Danny. In my view, both were "inspired" by a poor facsimile of love in the heart of the priest or perpetrator, an emotion borne more out of passion and obsession than out of love and wonder.

Not that evening, but shortly afterward, I met with Carter in the visiting room of the jail. The room was furnished with rows of tables with dividers so minimal as to be symbolic, a barrier not to be transgressed (according to a sign on the wall) under the watchful eyes of the guards. Though there was no window between us, only air, I would not be allowed to employ my usual practice of reaching to touch the hands of the person I counseled or with whom I prayed. I expected to find Carter morose, introspective, and guilty. But he was his characteristic outgoing self, cracking wise about his "accommodations" and "fellow guests." This would be his M.O. during our entire relationship, but with intervals in which he told me the truth, or as much of the truth as he cared to offer or knew himself, during which he revealed the sadness, pathos, and a darker reality underlying his comic and dramatic fantasy world.

A lawyer had taken up his case *pro bono*, though Carter had to sign over his life possessions. I wondered if Carter's soul were included in the bargain, as the lawyer was both famous and infamous, himself in the news at the time for allegedly bribing judges. The next year was filled with aborted trial dates as his lawyer, according to Carter, played the game of repeatedly requesting a continuance in court appearances (if he showed at all), a ploy used to eventually discredit witnesses whose memories fail after a year's time (or, if their memories remain intact, being maligned on the witness stand for "too perfect" recollection). I was present in court for each trial date to be supportive of Carter. Much to everyone's amazement, Carter was released on his own recognizance (no bail!) shortly before Christmas of that year. His friends theorized that Carter was released because of the nefarious manipulations of the judicial system by his defense attorney.

Subsequently, Carter and I would often drive over to the courtroom together and, after the nth postponement, would sometimes take lunch together. He introduced me to dim sum in nearby Chinatown; and I introduced him to my favorite Chinese dive, the L.A. China Kitchen on Sunset in Silver Lake. It was a mom-and-pop restaurant, at the time having what seemed like former bus seats for seating. The sardonically humorous waitress was the cook's wife. She knew me well, and would kid me each time she "reluctantly" waited on me. When Carter and I ate there, he broke down and cried, prompting the waitress to come over to me and joke in her broken English, "What with you? Ever'body you bring here, you make cry!" Indeed, two other people I had brought there had broken down while we talked over a meal. One had just lost her father. The other had lost a relationship. Carter had lost everything, except the will to survive at any cost, a theme his therapist in the jail wing of the hospital had drilled into him. "No matter what you've done," she had told him plainly, "Now you have to do your best to survive." And he did, even through two incidents which brought him close to death. One occurred when he became suicidal, and Ron called to ask me to talk some sense into him. I rushed to his apartment and sat with him for a long time that night, convincing him both he and his friends deserved better, reminding him of his therapist's advice to survive, until he calmed down and felt like he could sleep. Another came when he suffered an intestinal hemorrhage and nearly bled to death. I rushed to intensive care to offer him comfort only to find him delivering his usual comic performance, lay-down rather than stand-up comedy, comforting his visitors and cracking up his nurses.

The evidence was mounting against Carter. The notes he wrote suggested premeditation, because they were dated the day before the murder. Carter claimed, in his confusion after the murder, to have posted the wrong date on the letters. The struggle for the gun was believable, but the fact that Carter had purchased it just two weeks before again implied premeditation. With me Carter was usually vaguely mysterious. One reason was that I might be called as a character witness, and the less I knew, the better. Perhaps, too, he feared I would not be as supportive if I knew the whole truth. But the most important reason, I believe, is that Carter obfuscated reality in his own mind—in other words, the less he himself knew, the better. That, plus his diminished capacity due to the drugs he had shot into his veins, made a lucid memory nearly impossible. There had been some thought for arguing diminished capacity, a practical strategy I endorsed while also believing ultimately it did not entirely acquit the guilt of a perpetrator because I believe a perpetrator has to take responsibility for ingesting drugs or alcohol in the first place. I believe it was during the time of finally selecting members of the jury that, during the lunch break, Carter and I went walking around downtown Los Angeles and, purposely beside a roaring water fountain, Carter told me exactly what had happened, his words drowned for others to hear, including the reader, by the sound of crashing water.

Carter had plenty of character witnesses, so he had persuaded his attorney not to call me, thus affording me the opportunity to proceed with a long-planned Fordham University religious studies tour of the Middle East. Upon my return, church member Lynn McClary picked me up at the airport and informed me that Carter had been convicted of murder in the *first degree*, to my great surprise, and sentenced to 25-years-to-life. In prison, Carter got a boyfriend named "Tink," a good clerk's job in the warden's office, and became a proficient artist, displaying his drawings and water colors, often of flowers, in art shows, and sending them to friends. In the year leading up to his trial, Carter had become a favorite with the members of my church, and so we sent quarterly "care packages" (as frequently as was allowed by prison rules) that fulfilled Carter's exquisite and exotic if not downright pretentious "wish lists" that included, as I recall, rare cheeses and caviar. His brief incarceration in the Los Angeles County Jail had revealed that gay inmates were not allowed to go to the chaplain's services unless they signed a paper confessing their homosexuality as sin, so a member of our church spearheaded weekly worship services on the gay cell block. Carter became a prolific letter writer, and soon the number of his correspondents (many of whom never knew him before he went to prison) prompted him to send out a periodic newsletter. He often had visitors. I saw him once in San Quentin on a visit to San Francisco. But my finances were such that I could not visit him otherwise, and I must confess I was an unreliable correspondent.

His 25-years-to-life ultimately proved to be a death sentence. He became infected with HIV, common in prisons, and he ultimately died trying to medicate himself, to make up for the lack of prison medical care. A manuscript about prison life on which he'd been working mysteriously disappeared upon his passing, and most of his friends assumed the prison guards or hierarchy had destroyed it, if it existed at all. I led a memorial service for him at the church, and more than half of those attending only had known him since his incarceration!

Years later, in an argument with a new acquaintance about the death penalty (he was for it and I was opposed), he asked if I had ever been the victim of violent crime as he himself had been. As a teenager, I had once been attacked by a gang before my brother interceded, saving me from any real harm. But I had to confess I had not. I explained I did have friends who had been assaulted, even killed. Then I thought to ask him: had he ever known anyone on trial for murder who could be given the death penalty? Had he suffered with anyone who could die as a result of a momentary, single, ill-considered act? Though I had previously opposed the death penalty, my experience with Carter demonstrated to me how pointless "a life for a life" was as a policy. It not only makes *us* killers, changing our better nature, but also desecrates and disallows the spiritually vital virtues of confession, forgiveness, redemption, and atonement. Even on a surface level, to kill Carter would have been a waste of a life still able to bring others laughter, pleasure, and purpose; thus diminishing us all. The same wrath that makes us want to kill the perpetrators of violent acts should fuel our resistance to society performing such acts itself. But would I feel the same toward someone who would never contribute to society in a healthy way, who could probably never be redeemed? Would I feel the same toward someone who killed a close personal friend or family member? The closer brushes with murder that followed would serve as a test.

The Murder of a Colleague

Dick Hetz was a tall man with hidden strength and visible gentleness. He had served as a pastor until entrapped by an undercover vice cop in a gay bar in the days when police would arrest anyone merely extending an invitation, even in their own sanctuaries. Dick was forced out of ministry and became a salesman for an upscale Beverly Hills office furniture store. His wife, emotionally troubled all her life, took her own life by hanging herself from a crossbeam in the basement, to be discovered one afternoon by their two sons upon their return home from school. Her suicide was believed unrelated to Dick's sexuality, confirmed by the fact that her family never faulted Dick and kept closer ties to him than his own family. His sons grew up and both inherited his gay genes, the older becoming an architect and the younger becoming an artist. The younger died of cancer at the tender age of twenty-six in the family home where Dick cared for him.

Though Dick kept his ordination and membership in the Presbyterian Church, he only returned to Presbyterian worship when I was on staff of West Hollywood Presbyterian Church. Concerned with the aesthetics of the worship experience, Dick would bring cuttings from his yard almost weekly, fashioning tasteful wooden pedestals for the vases which held them in the raised chancel area of the sanctuary. He gave exquisite dinner parties that welcomed intriguing conversation, punctuated by insight and humor. Between Christmas and New Year's Eve he invited the entire church (we were small then) to his home for a champagne "white elephant" party, which was the social highlight of the year for many of us. When Ross Greek, the pastor with whom I served, retired, many of us hoped Dick would return to active ministry and become pastor of our church. He insisted that I was his pastor, so my job description was rewritten and Dick was retained to do things only an ordained minister could do, such as moderate the Session (governing elders of a congregation) and administer the sacraments of baptism and Holy Communion.

My first long-term relationship was with Tom, a man who thought of himself as bisexual at the time. He couldn't commit to me, and eventually married Ann, a longtime sweetheart that he had kept hidden from me during the entire time of our relationship. When I officially met Ann, having unofficially met her one evening when she showed up unannounced at Tom's, we liked each other immediately. She had been trying to persuade Tom to marry for awhile. They had even obtained a marriage license. To accomplish the union, Ann knew it would have to be brief in the preparation, so one morning I received a call from her asking if Dick might be available that evening to do the ceremony. Tom and Ann were married in Dick's home with friends of theirs, a straight couple, and me as witnesses, along with Ann's poodle. For their wedding gift, I took the whole party out for dinner at a nice East Hollywood Italian restaurant that boasted waiters who sang opera. It was great fun.

One month later, Ann's mother, the "Rona Barrett" of Palm Springs television, gave a fashionable wedding reception on a Saturday afternoon for her friends at a swanky desert country club. Dick was to give the invocation, but he never showed up, nor did he call anyone, atypically. We all wondered what had happened, but went on with the celebration. Afterward a few of their friends continued the party at the condo where Ann and Tom were staying. I was with Bob Barnes, a comedian I was dating at the time, and together we drove home to Los Angeles, arriving late in the evening. Walking into my apartment, I noticed my answering machine had reached its maximum of twenty messages. I sensed immediately something was wrong, but before I could rewind the tape to play the messages, the phone rang. I picked it up, and it was my mother's voice, quite anxious. "You haven't heard?" she judged from the sound of my voice. "Everyone's been trying to reach you. Dick Hetz has been murdered, stabbed to death"—which was as close as my mother could come to saying "his throat was slit." I report it here as if I am certain exactly what she said in making the announcement. I know for sure she remarked with surprise "you haven't heard?" but whether she first said Dick had been murdered or stabbed, I have no memory. I do remember my legs gave way beneath me and I was on the floor, at the same time annoyed at my body's drama. Gradually I grasped what she was telling me, how members of the church had been trying to reach me all day since the body was discovered, that the body was discovered because the murderer had attempted to set Dick's house on fire. I was grateful Bob was with me. I played the messages: distraught and grieving voices all, with one exception of a call for something that, in another context, would have seemed important, but now struck me as exceedingly mundane. Death contextualizes, even may trivialize everything else; a violent death even more so. I returned the calls I could, given the lateness of the hour.

I tossed out Sunday morning's sermon. Most people in the congregation had heard the news or were hearing it as we gathered for worship. Only those who timed their arrival close or came in late were shocked to hear it in the opening announcements. I reflected on Dick's death during the time set aside for the sermon, and then opened the conversation to the gathered community. Much pain and confusion were expressed. The confusion came from those having difficulty wrapping their minds around a violent death for anyone close to them, let alone such a peaceful man of God. Ron Larason, whose former roommate Carter had been implicated in the murder earlier described, explained later that just as he had begun to trust God again, Dick's murder called all into question again. Was God in control or not? Many who thought of me as too young to be their pastoral figure had revered Dick in that role, the father-figure whose affirmation they sought, and an authority to be believed when he told them that they were good, that God loved them.

What later surfaced was many congregants' anger. This is not unusual in the case of violent crime. Nor is it unusual for such anger to be displaced on such people as medical personnel, police investigators, or morticians. What was unique was *how* their anger was displaced, directed not at the one who allegedly took Dick's life, but ironically, toward the denomination that had originally denied Dick's livelihood as a minister. To channel this anger, I would later suggest that people in the congregation write personal letters telling their own stories of church rejection to Presbyterian leaders in the Los Angeles area. One playwright in the church began writing a play about Dick and his death that, I heard secondhand, was a bit of a hagiography. Having been unjustly transmuted into the eternal realm activated the phenomenon of which I wrote earlier, the effective sainthood of the dead, especially of those whose lives have been taken prematurely or unfairly. Yet death's canonization in this case seemed to confirm what we already knew about him. It also made me glad I had not confronted him during a conference we had the night before his murder about something in our working relationship that was disturbing me. Even now I am loathe to admit that I was angry with him, even though I held my peace. Death transforms some of our most ordinary meetings into final encounters, reminding us that every rendezvous should end on the best possible terms. The friend who was with me when I learned of Dick's death, Bob Barnes, bore a tremendous burden of guilt for one of the last things he said to his mother before her death: "I wish you were dead!" A typical expression of teenage rebellion, expressed in ignorance of his mother's proximity to death, became a source of self-recrimination for the rest of his life. Even, or perhaps especially, saints can make one angry; best to remember another's sacred worth in the midst of any clash.

Yet our saint had died in an unsaintly, unseemly manner. He had picked someone up along Santa Monica Boulevard and brought him home for dinner. Most of what follows is based on the suspect's bragging to friends who became "hostile witnesses" for the prosecution. After dinner, they had had sex "all over the house." Then the suspect had tied Dick up, presumably at the point of a gun, wanting money and valuables and the access code to his bankcard. He slashed Dick's throat. Dick begged for his life, urging him to take what he wanted and go, maybe call for help. Because Dick "wasn't dying fast enough," the suspect took a pillow to muffle a shot to Dick's brain. He set several fires throughout the house and drove off with Dick's car. The fires alerted the neighbors to trouble, and they called the fire department. The next day the suspect was apprehended by police after trying to use one of Dick's credit cards, thanks to a smart clerk who thought the name "Hetz" sounded Jewish and the man trying to use the card was African-American. He was still driving Dick's green convertible. Most of those attending subsequent court proceedings withheld from others the fact that the suspect was black, for fear of inflaming people's prejudice. What's interesting to me, though I've decided to exclude it from this account, is that I remember his name so clearly after all these years, a person I only saw once; when I would be hard-pressed to recall some of the names of friends from that period.

The one time I saw the suspect was at the pre-trial hearing during which a decision is made whether there is enough evidence to go to trial. What I saw chilled me. He seemed to me to be one of those sociopaths so shaped by life circumstances that he had no conscience, no ability to grasp what he had done as wrong, no emotion that would prompt him to care. Photographs were presented showing Dick's corpse on the ground, the pockets of the slacks he wore pulled inside out, evidence of the suspect rifling through for valuables. Now as I write this I wonder why Dick was clothed if indeed they had had sex "all over the house"? Was this just a homophobic play for sympathy, a bid perhaps to claim "homosexual panic" during the subsequent trial? I don't know because I never went to the trial, partly because I had had my fill at the pre-trial, and partly because this was how I expressed my grief and anger. I wanted to have nothing to do with this person who killed my friend. The leader of our jail ministry admitted being haunted a little by the possibility that Dick's killer could be among those attending our weekly worship services in the gay cell block. Church members who did attend the trial kept us informed. After his conviction, several of us, including Dick's son Scott, wrote the judge asking the death penalty not be given—in the spirit of the victim, who opposed the death penalty. "Special circumstances"— in this case, robbery—warranted capital punishment in California. Ultimately, the suspect was given a relatively short period of incarceration instead.

Introduced as evidence at the pre-trial hearing was an empty silver box found in Dick's living room with the suspect's fingerprints, conclusively placing him at the scene of the crime. I knew immediately what it was. During a break in the proceedings, the prosecuting attorney, knowing we were from Dick's church, came over to us waving the box, now in a plastic bag. "Any idea what this may have contained?" he asked us. "A wedding gift," I said. "He was supposed to attend a marriage reception Saturday afternoon."

Of course all of this happened weeks later. It was but a day or two after Dick's death that I met Scott at his father's Silver Lake house, near the base of the reservoir pocketed between foothills that characterize that Los Angeles neighborhood. Scott had broken the police crime scene tape to enter. He escorted me through the living room, smelling of and smudged by smoke from the fires the murderer had set to cover his deed. I passed by the self-portrait of the other son, my favorite of the son's paintings, peering at us through blades of grass as he lounged chest down on a lawn, his left cheek resting on the backs of his hands. Then we walked through the dining area, past the dining table on which remained the china, silver, and wine goblets used for dinner. Even with a stranger Dick had been stylishly hospitable, a gift he solemnly brought to his celebration of the Eucharist for our congregation. The clutter now strewn throughout the house, particularly in the bedroom, revealed the thief's desperate attempt to uncover something of value. An open armoire disclosed something priceless: a box that held the ashes of Dick's other son. He had never buried the ashes, and had once explained to me with a self-deprecating smile that he found it comforting from time to time to speak to him there.

Scott led me past the door that opened to the basement where he and his brother had found his mother so very long ago, out to the patio surrounded by the garden Dick had carefully tended and where Dick's body apparently had been found or moved, at least, according to the photos we saw later of the crime scene. There we sat at a wrought iron and glass table around which Dick entertained in the cool of summer evenings, and there I learned for the first time that this was the same house in which the mother and other son had died. The pathos of being the sole surviving member of the family showed on Scott's face. Little did I know that, a few years hence, the relatively young and vigorous Scott too would pass, falling victim to a chance blood infection that took his vitality in days. He and his partner had made pre-need arrangements, but in anticipation that his lover, infected with HIV, would precede his HIV-negative partner in death. A cliché, I know, but death is truly fickle. The whole family together.

But this future was not merely furthest from our thoughts; it wasn't even in our thoughts that day as we reflected together on the family tragedies that had occurred in this Eden-like environment. Scott was covering his emotions by being philosophic, but we also discussed the practical. Scott wanted to see his father's body before it was cremated, and I agreed to accompany him to Forest Lawn, the first of two times I would see and touch the unprepared but thoroughly-chilled body of a loved one at a branch of the famous cemetery's chain. Scott's partner, Jim, had joined us by that time; and both of them kissed Dick on the forehead, a touching farewell gesture. I was not ready for such intimacy with the dead. I placed my hands, one on his hand, the other on his forehead, remarkably unblemished by what must have been a rear entry bullet wound. The gash on his neck must have been covered by the white cotton sheet that wrapped the rest of his body, for I did not see it.

Outside on the green grounds surrounding the Tudor-style mortuary in Glendale, we met the organist of Dick's former church, Helen Sloss, to plan the funeral. Helen seemed very old even then, wise and sparkling blue eyes framed by the translucent skin and stark white hair of later years, and every time I've seen her since, I've been very much surprised to find her still alive and kicking, an ongoing joke between us. "You still alive?" I kid her. As we considered what hymns to use she piped up that she knew which hymn *not* to use. "He hated 'In the Garden,'" she said, "That sweet 'me and Jesus' sentimentality." I remembered it fondly from my childhood Baptist church:

> *I come to the garden alone,*
> *While the dew is still on the roses,*
> *And the voice I hear, falling on my ear,*
> *The Son of God discloses.*
> *And he walks with me and he talks with me,*
> *And he tells me I am his own.*
> *And the joy we share as we tarry there*
> *None other has ever known.*

I loved the old song. It had been at least played, if not sung, at the funerals of many of my relatives. But, in good humor, Helen brought me back into the reality of Dick's intellectually muscular faith, tender and sweet as he was. "If he was late starting the worship service," she explained mischievously, "I would just segue from the prelude into that hymn, and he'd be lickety-split in the chancel ready to begin."

Dick's funeral service would draw more than two-hundred people, more than the fire department would have permitted in our small sanctuary if it had known. Because of a foul-up, he had not yet been cremated, so his body was delivered in a beautiful, closed cherry wood coffin. Scott later quipped that if his dad had seen it, he would have exclaimed, "Now that would make a dandy table!" Dick was constantly recycling things, transforming them from their original purpose.

I gave the talk, a cross between a eulogy and a meditation. I entitled it "The Importance of Flowers," and I described Dick's care tending not only his own garden but our chancel, decorating it with fresh flowers and cuttings, and on Palm Sunday, with palms he had gathered "assisting" freeway road crews keeping on-ramps trimmed. But I also spoke how this flower had been crushed by a church for his sexuality, angering some people from the presbytery (our denomination's regional unit) who, in their patronizing way, thought Dick had been treated "kindly," while removing him from his pastorate! Scott was delighted with my honesty; the minister, Ross Greek, with whom I had worked before his retirement, was furious. I was surprised especially by his angry reaction, as I had not done this to make a political statement, just to reflect on the meaning of Dick's life for all those gathered, especially considering the anger the congregation now felt toward the Presbyterian Church. Shy and retiring himself, Dick had rarely spoken of his hurt and anger and frustration with the church, and only to me and a few intimates.

I don't believe death is a time to reveal all secrets, but I do believe death may serve as an occasion to surface truths that may reform hearts. In his letters to his brother Theo, Vincent van Gogh described life as a kind of sowing time, the harvest of which may not come in our lifetimes. Surely that was true of his own "seeds"—his paintings—which would only be appreciated after his own passing. Theologian Reinhold Niebuhr wrote in *The History of Christianity*, "Nothing that is worth doing can be achieved in our lifetime; therefore we must be saved by hope. Nothing which is true or beautiful or good makes complete sense in any immediate context of history; therefore we must be saved by faith. Nothing we do, however virtuous, can be accomplished alone; therefore we must be saved by love." Dick had left behind in us seeds of hope, faith, and love. More broadly, many of those who have passed have left behind in us seeds of hope, faith, and love. Death urges us to tend our gardens so these seeds may grow and blossom and bear fruit for others. The fruits we offer others contain seeds themselves; as they die, the earth is replenished with yet more seeds. Eventually there should be enough to feed the world.

In his book *New Seeds of Contemplation*, Catholic mystic Thomas Merton wrote, "Every moment and every event of every man's life on earth plants something in his soul. For just as the wind carries thousands of winged seeds, so each moment brings with it germs of spiritual vitality that come to rest imperceptibly in the minds and wills of men. Most of these unnumbered seeds perish and are lost, because men are not prepared to receive them: for such seeds as these cannot spring up anywhere except in the good soil of freedom, spontaneity and love." The final conformity, Death casts us back upon ourselves to find the "freedom, spontaneity and love" that makes life not only possible but meaningful. Jean Paul Sartre's understanding of death as the ultimate confinement wherein others can make of you what they wish, exercising total control over the deceased, underlined the necessity for his existentialist philosophy. "Carpe diem" before it "carpes" you.

A Friend's Murder

On the morning of his fortieth birthday, I took Scott Rogo out for breakfast at a bright and trendy Melrose café in West Hollywood. Eyes twinkling happily through his glasses, he leaned back in a wood chair, a knowing smile beneath his coarse mustache and small but stern nose, and told me he was ready for the next stage of his life. He had applied for a position with an AIDS agency, ready to transition from a writer of some thirty tomes investigating the paranormal to an AIDS educator, something I personally witnessed he did very well as a part-time volunteer. I wondered if he would sell his typewriter to "finalize the deal" as he had sold his musical instrument when he successfully weaned himself from a musical to a writing career. His last music gigs were as a substitute violinist for the Honolulu Philharmonic. Little did he know how prophetic his words about a new era in his life would be.

Enya's popular song about the unpredictability of where time will lead comes to mind as I think of the twists in our separate paths that led to our unique friendship. I suppose that could be said of any friendship, but ours came in a serendipitous and circuitous fashion that would have shocked our earlier selves. We vaguely knew each other at John H. Francis Polytechnic High School in the San Fernando Valley, a suburban part of Los Angeles. As I've already written, I was in the school choir. He was next door in band. I was very religious. He had disdain for most things religious, or perhaps I should say, for religious people. This contrast became even clearer during my first semester at California State University at Northridge when I discovered him, to my dismay, in the same "Man's Religions" course offered by the just-established Religious Studies Department. Taught by United Methodist minister Dr. Thomas Love, it challenged much of what I had been taught by my own religion, including its exclusivistic claims as well as how to read the Bible. To have an often caustic Scott Rogo expressing his skepticism in our class discussions added to my discomfort. At the time, I didn't know if he remembered me from high school (he did), as we never spoke directly. Only of the discussion on death do I remember a distinct quote of his during class, probably arising from his then unknown-to-me discovery of the paranormal, initiated by an out-of-body experience (an "O.B.E.") as a teenager and developed by his broad reading and research on the paranormal, which led him to publish his first book before he graduated from high school. After one student confessed his fear of death, Scott had said, "I'm looking forward to my death. I think it will be a fascinating experience." This statement was stunning to me, to say the least, especially coming from one who held no traditional religious concepts of the afterlife.

In the nearly two decades between that class and our later friendship, I remember only one or two occasions when I heard his voice, both times being interviewed on late night radio, once about a book he co-wrote with Raymond Bayless entitled, *Phone Calls from the Dead.* Though I remain skeptical, I would learn that many have reported such paranormal communication that most often occurs, if I remember correctly, as or just after a loved one has died. Scott must have heard me either on a radio program or seen me on television, because he knew of my work, providing the link that eventually brought us together.

(Subsequent to the publication of *Phone Calls,* one of Scott's friends, a practical joker, mischievously circulated a rumor that Scott was looking for material for a sequel entitled, *Faxes from the Dead,* which undoubtedly would have been followed in this day and age by *E-Mails from the Dead.* I myself once received a letter from the dead, causing considerable shock. It came from Henry Kuizenga, a seminary professor and religious writer who was a friend. He had been murdered and robbed in a closeted encounter, and I had already attended his memorial service when the letter arrived, sent by his wife, who found it in his things. I was disappointed to find its contents were not momentous, given the circumstances.)

The pastor with whom I worked toward the end of my time at West Hollywood Presbyterian Church, the Rev. Dan Smith, passed along a note to me from Scott, whom he met during a training session for volunteers at AIDS Project Los Angeles. Scott's note reminded me of our high school and college connections, explained that he had heard of my work, and wondered if I might like to meet for lunch. I was surprised. I did not know Scott was gay, yet that seemed to be the reason for the connection, given that most people concerned about AIDS at the time were. I had reservations, but my curiosity made me eager to arrange lunch and we did, and thus began my only regularly-scheduled lunch, once a fortnight. Often we met at the French Market Place on Santa Monica Boulevard, though we also tried other places along the main boulevard of West Hollywood.

Right away, at our first meeting, we laughed at our earlier dissonance over religion. Scott explained his work as a parapsychologist, a skeptic and debunker of most so-called paranormal activity, but enough of a believer that he was assured of life beyond what met our eyes on this plane of experience. Myself a believer from the perspective of faith, I found it refreshing to regularly encounter someone who "believed" from the perspective of empirical evidence. Scott seemed more respectful of religion than he had been earlier, eventually visiting the church where I worked, but realizing it did not do for him what his home synagogue accomplished, though he rarely attended the latter. I eagerly read some of his books, and he as eagerly served as one of the readers of the manuscript of my first book, *Uncommon Calling.* He was the one who suggested its title when Harper & Row, its first publisher, rejected mine. He also made another vital contribution. Though Jewish, he appreciated that, as he described it, throughout the book, "Every crucifixion is followed by a resurrection. And yet the book ends with a 'crucifixion.' You need to end with a resurrection." Thus I added an epilogue that underlined the meaning of what had gone before and expressed the hope of what would come.

Scott preferred our lunch arrangement to dinners together or dinner parties. He had "shy ways," though he traveled the world giving talks on the paranormal. Only once did he accept an invitation to a dinner party that George Lynch and I hosted. And only once did he invite us to dinner, though the reason was primarily to watch an interesting foreign film he had recorded about which he wanted our reflections. The film, *Man Facing Southeast,* was about a Christ-like figure committed to a mental institution in Argentina who believed he came from another galaxy, and whose powers and compassion make his therapist wonder at the plausibility. A film with a similar concept, *K-PAX,* was made later in the U.S. starring Kevin Spacey. (Scott would also tape for me a copy of the classic film *The Bishop's Wife* which became one of my two favorite holiday films.)

Man Facing Southeast was provocative, but I was more intrigued seeing Scott's living and writing space. It was my only visit to his home. I asked to see where he wrote, and he led us into a room in the heart of the house with shelves of books lining two walls and paneling on the other two, hung with framed covers of his books. Scott had had the windows covered up so he would have no outside distractions. In the center of the room was a plain wooden table which held an old manual typewriter. It looked like something from the 1930's, not unlike one on which I had learned to type. I was shocked to discover Scott had written each of his thirty books on this typewriter—shocked, because I had always assumed he worked on a computer or word processor, or at the least, on an electric typewriter as I did when I wrote my first book. The final manuscript of each book would be retyped by his mother at his father's C.P.A. office before it was sent off to the publisher. That evening in his home was pleasant but awkward. Scott was clearly not used to entertaining, and it felt strange being in his home. We never did it again.

In 1987, Scott phoned me. He was finishing work on his twenty-seventh work, *The Infinite Boundary*. He told me that the book's dedication had come to him in a sudden flash of insight: he had decided to dedicate the book to me! "You're my only friend who initiates our times together just as I do. And the book has a Presbyterian minister as a major character," he explained. Up to that time, I don't think I completely realized how much our friendship meant to him. I was deeply touched. When the book was published, there it was on the dedication page: "TO CHRIS GLASER—In appreciation for his past and future ministry." At the time, the book's subtitle didn't bother me— "A Psychic Look at Spirit Possession, Madness, and Multiple Personality"— though, as I write about it now, it elicits a smile to have a book about such things dedicated to me. Even so, to this day it is an honor to open to that page with my name standing alone.

Scott had been serving on the Spiritual Advisory Committee of AIDS Project Los Angeles, a committee of volunteers created to encourage care-receivers and care-givers alike to utilize spirituality as a resource in the AIDS crisis. In the days when APLA first had tiny offices in an apartment building, I had served, rather ineffectively, as volunteer co-chair of spiritual resources. Now there was this committee, and Scott asked me to take his place. I did, and with Rabbi Denise Eger, effectively co-led the committee of volunteers ranging from Baptists to Buddhists. We had a New Thought representative, but no New Age person as yet, and I had considered inviting James van Praagh to join our group. Scott and I happened to see him having lunch with an associate at the French Market during our regular lunch engagement, and Scott explained that James probably desired to avoid him: "James doesn't like me because he knows I think his talking to the dead is pure bunk." This was many years before James was known, having yet to write his *New York Times* bestseller-listed books and before his appearance on various television programs or the production of the made-for-TV miniseries about him featuring Ted Danson as James himself! Scott went on to describe how psychics can use their gift to read people to fool the public and how little he thought of such practice. I was surprised by this evaluation from someone who specialized in studies of the paranormal; but it revealed how Scott approached his material: with skeptical scientific scrutiny.

I was a little more open-minded, though I was afraid James could read my own doubts every time we met. Yet I did want a New Age representative on the committee. And he seemed to use his powers, whatever their nature, for good. He thought of himself as a Christian, and applied those principles to his work. Many years later, as his fame spread, his credibility increased in my view by virtue of his positive association with longtime friends of mine, friends who were not as certain of his gifts as of his sincerity in helping people.

It's easy for people with more traditional spiritualities to judge someone like James, but frankly, all spiritualities contain an element of "whistling in the dark" or "wishful thinking" as Frederick Buechner has characterized it in the titles of two of his books. We believe in something because the alternative is too terrible. The contrasting nihilism sported by some of the younger generations is more style than substance, as I've already opined, though enough of it becomes substantial to cause real destruction. Perhaps theirs is more a loss of imagination than of faith. In *Care of the Soul*, Thomas Moore asserts that imagination is one of the most underestimated and underutilized spiritual gifts. To imagine that everything fits together somehow, that every event carries meaning, is the imagination of faith. It's like a net that captures everything, holds it all together, and catches us as we fall. Its rationalist equivalent is the quest for a theory of everything, an elusive holy grail among scientists.

From Christian tradition, two metaphors come to mind: a metaphysical net to make Jesus' followers fishers of men and women; and a new wineskin in which to put the fresh wine of a new faith. Notice both net and new wineskin suggest flexibility. A net has an ability to stretch around something, around people and experiences highly diverse; a wineskin has an ability to stretch as the wine ferments, giving off its gasses, transforming its nature into something intoxicating. Spiritual imagination stretches around the events of our lives and spiritual communities, catching up everything into a context of meaning, facilitating the focus that growth requires, transforming our nature in spiritual ecstasy (in the sense of "out of stasis," beyond the status quo).

Talking with the dead requires just a little bit more imagination than speaking or praying to the dead. Many of us speak to our dead fathers or mothers, spouses or children, from time to time, or pray to saints who are believed to minister to various needs. And many pray for the dead, from moving them out of purgatory to simply remembering them with love. While I doubt James van Praagh's ability to speak with the dead, maybe it's a question of my having less imagination than he does.

All of this came into play shortly after I made a phone call home from the Detroit airport in August 1990 to report a several-hour delay in my return to Los Angeles from Toronto. There was something in George's voice that made me ask, "What's wrong?" When he told me he'd tell me when I got home, I exclaimed, "Don't leave me hanging all the way from Detroit to L.A.!" He told me Scott had been killed, stabbed to death in his home. He had learned of it from a friend at church that morning, who had read of it in the paper. Standing at a public phone on a wide stretch of monotonous tile floor in the Detroit airport, I wanted to sink but could not. After hanging up the phone, overwhelmed by grief, I wanted a private place to cry. There's no sanctuary for strong feelings in an airport. So I stuffed it, but stuffing it made me too restless to sit or read.

Suddenly a phone began to ring along the bank of phones on the opposite side of the corridor from where I was standing, still by the phone on which I had received the sad news. My immediate thought was someone had failed to insert enough coins, and the operator was ringing in the phone company's idealized expectation that a customer would feel compelled to answer the phone and pay up. But then I realized that no one had been using those phones while I had been talking to George. Scott's book, *Phone Calls from the Dead*, came to mind, and, disbelieving, a wry smile came to my face as I considered, "What if it's Scott?" I walked across the hallway and answered the phone. No one was on the line. At least, no one I could hear. Only silence. I smiled at my own imagination.

In contrast to their investigation of my other friend's murder, with which I began this chapter, the police were more thorough in investigating Scott's murder. Scott's body had been found when a neighbor reported a yard sprinkler that had been left on for more than a day. The investigating detective called me for any information I could offer, as well as to verify my own whereabouts during the time of the murder. I told him of a person Scott had mentioned once, about whom I had expressed concern at the time. Scott described occasional assignations with a bodybuilder who claimed he was straight. I had explained my fear to Scott that the bodybuilder might someday turn on him in the so-called "justification" for anti-gay violence and brutal murders known as "homosexual panic." This turned out to be a significant lead, but not as helpful to the case as the work of a psychic. The psychic had been brought into the case through a woman friend of Scott's who would not let the case die, a devoted fan who so believed in Scott's work that she interviewed almost everyone who knew him, including me, risking the reputation of becoming "that crazy lady" among his friends. The psychic she brought into the case told police to check the glasses in the kitchen cupboards for fingerprints. Scott was known to be fastidious, washing used glasses immediately after their use. One glass held the fingerprint of the bodybuilder, who had apparently put it away the day of the murder. The fingerprint, when combined with discrepancies in the testimonies between his girlfriend and himself, both of whom had returned from Hawai'i the very day of the murder, led to his conviction. A fingerprint in blood of a second suspect could not be traced. Apparently one held Scott while the other stabbed him. Because Scott carried only small sums of money at any given time, the motive apparently was anger that he could not produce enough money so they could buy drugs.

So segmented was Scott's life that I was never informed of services for him at his synagogue, and I only knew of his friends at AIDS Project Los Angeles, where I initiated and led a memorial service with a dozen friends with whom he had served on the HIV/AIDS hotline and speaker's bureau. I'm not sure how or why Scott's parents and I began to communicate, which is how Scott's father came to be at our little service. Perhaps it was because I was one of four friends mentioned in his will, for which his father served as executor. This sign of the value Scott placed on our friendship caught me by surprise. It also served as serendipitous support of a fellow writer, for I had recently left church employment to write and speak full time. The bulk of his estate naturally went to his parents, but the equal sums bequeathed to four friends suggested not only his gratitude but the compartmentalization of his life, as I did not know the other three. Soon his mother phoned with a nagging doubt. Apparently she had learned from his papers that he was gay. Plaintively she fished for assurance, "He surely knew we would accept him as gay, didn't he?" I gladly assured her. We had discussed why he had not come out to his parents, and he had indicated he believed they would be supportive, but questioned the need to complicate their relationship with "too much information," as we call it these days.

Scott left his library to a school where he had taught parapsychology, John F. Kennedy University in Orinda, California. I urged his father to persuade the school to take Scott's typewriter too, as a kind of historical relic. When they declined, he gave it to me. As I later told friends the story, I would speculate whether Scott might try to communicate through it, a kind of "Correspondence from the Dead"! One friend made the obvious suggestion that I put a sheet of paper in it, but the page remained blank, and when I moved to Atlanta three years later, I guiltily pondered leaving the typewriter behind. Suddenly, I could almost hear Scott saying, "Chuck it!" He would be the last to carry or have others carry on his behalf what he would have considered dead weight.

Scott had believed he was about to enter a new stage in his life, though perhaps not one quite so "fascinating," as the death he had anticipated in college. As far as I know, he's not phoned from the dead, nor spoken with James van Praagh, but he continues to speak through his writings. Without religious and dogmatic rhetoric, he still gives his readers—as he personally gave me, in life and in death—an empirical glimpse of what may lie beyond what meets the eye, a spark of hope that this is not, as Peggy Lee used to sing, all there is.

Chapter Four
Transforming Deaths

During high school I identified with a Peanuts comic strip featuring Snoopy, who was trying to resist falling in love with yet another snowman with coal eyes, stick arms, and a carrot nose. Snoopy thinks something like, "I know you'll melt and leave me high and dry!" Unable to help himself, he gives in, lovingly throwing his paws around the snowman's icy middle. To Snoopy's alarm, the sun comes out, and he watches in dismay as his friend slowly melts away like all the others. "Auuughhh . . . !!" comes the anguished cry of grief. From the window, Charlie Brown comments to Linus about how sensitive Snoopy is. Linus replies, "But not too sensitive to eat the carrot."

That's me. I hate, I grieve, the loss of relationships. But I am pragmatic enough "to eat the carrot" left behind—that is, finding what remains that is nourishing, whether as comforting memory or as spiritual formation. This whole book is about "eating the carrots." Some carrots are as mystically transforming as a Eucharist, while others are simply nourishing like a meal. This chapter is devoted to those deaths, whether of people or relationships, that have offered me redemption, resurrection, atonement—at-one-ment with who I am, who I am called to be, and "who" is calling.

The death of a cousin and the death of a relationship very painfully taught me, for example, how vital "home" was to me. My cousin, Marjorie McCormick, spent her professional career in the record industry, mostly in public relations, but, on occasion, writing and producing her own songs. She had a bout with cancer that took her breasts and eventually took her life. She died the first summer I was home from seminary. We learned she had died late one night, and I remember being on the phone with my sister, with my brother on the extension. My sister gave voice to all of our thoughts, "It just doesn't seem possible that she's gone." She meant this in the sense that she was "one of us," our family in California, not "back home" in the Midwest, and one of the children (though the oldest) of that family, a kind of peer. We had visited her earlier that day, and though difficult to grasp, it was clear she was near death. Our family had been denied access to her in recent months by her protective parents, who, in their half-denial and half-hope, had thought if she could only devote her energies to fighting the cancer, she would not die. The only reason I got to see her earlier that summer was that I paid a surprise visit when I returned home from Yale Divinity School. Marjorie took a while to primp before I was allowed to enter her bedroom. Wig and makeup in place, I saw a still-lovely Marjorie. But the figure I saw the day of her death so shocked me that, when she reached her hand to me as I entered the hospital room, I am ashamed to say, I did not take it. She looked little like my cousin, a few hairs on a swollen head where the cancer now invaded her brain. Only as we talked, her childlike voice speaking nostalgically of our shared memories in a dazed, dreamlike state, did it seem like the old Marjorie. At her request, malts were brought in, and we all sipped them together on that hot August day in her hospital room overlooking her beloved Hollywood, where she had kept an apartment before her illness brought her home to her parents in North Hollywood. In the hallway, Uncle Harry rather brusquely told me now was the time to pray for her. I heard accusation in his voice, though it may have simply been anguish, as if I, a seminarian, represented a God that could let Marjorie die. I plaintively said, "I *have* been praying." I did not really intend the tone of voice that came out of me to sound quite so defensive, as if I were being accused of not doing my job.

That night she died alone in that room. I was shocked her parents had not stayed with her, but then, they were exhausted from weeks at the hospital. After the late-night phone call, I put one of her 78s on the record player and thought the words all the more poignant in her death: "Don't send me roses, it only makes me blue, it only makes me know how far away I am from you." A minister from her church, the Church of Religious Science, led her open-casket funeral service at Forest Lawn. Smiling throughout the talk, as if this were the best possible outcome, he spoke of Marjorie moving to a higher plane of existence. My brother later said the minister made death sound so positive, it was a wonder we all didn't immediately join my cousin! I don't know about the "higher plane." But, given her pain and suffering, perhaps death was the best possible solution. Later I would learn that death may be experienced as a kind of healing. Certainly it is the only cure for the pain of an incurable illness borne by both the receiver and giver of care, as well as the only cure to the grief we bear throughout our lives.

Up to that moment, no death had had such an impact on me. I had a vivid dream in which I was Marjorie in that hospital bed, hemorrhaging on my right side. I awoke with such pain in my abdomen, a pain that persisted over the next several weeks, that I went to a doctor. He ordered upper and lower gastrointestinal x-rays, but they showed nothing. Talk about internalizing one's grief! Or was it terror facing death? When I returned to seminary, a friend and I actually shared a dream one night, each driving along a dark desert highway that stretched out before us into blackness as we passed a female figure in a blue chiffon dress walking down the middle of the road, looking like death. My cousin had composed and recorded a song called "The Long, Hard Road," and she had been buried in a blue chiffon dress. That we shared the dream added to the mystery of it all; we had only just begun our relationship in the fall following her death. What startled us awake was my companion's loud sleep-talking, saying, "Did you see that?!" And then we described our nearly identical dreams.

The Yale Health Plan allowed for short-term psychiatric counseling, so, that year, I took advantage of it. I wanted to know why Marjorie's death affected me so profoundly. What I learned about myself in the therapeutic relationship was that I suffered "separation anxiety." I had pushed my limits to go so far away from home for seminary in the first place, a continent away from family, friends, and the familiar. I had also left behind a boyfriend who refused to come with me. My cousin's death had brought this home to me—a relevant idiomatic phrase. It was such a spiritual "aha," that I remember subsequently being stunned to encounter my therapist in the Yale Coop. He lived in New Haven? I don't know where I thought he lived—New York, maybe?—but it was as if God were standing before me. I was speechless and mumbled a greeting and hurried away.

The only other time I took to therapy was ten years later after the death of a relationship in the early 1980's. I had been through break-ups before, but the one with Jim plunged me into such despair that I wanted to discern why it was so important to me. I mention both Marjorie's death and the breakup in the same breath, or rather, page, because they are related in what they taught me about my need for home. Jim's and my relationship was only five months old when I went, with his encouragement, on another Fordham University religious studies tour, this time to India, Sri Lanka, and Nepal. On the trip, I was homesick for Jim, eager to see him when I flew home to Los Angeles. Instead, my parents greeted me at the airport, and I learned that Jim was in Hawai'i. I knew something was wrong, especially when I learned Jim had gone to Maui, where we had enjoyed such a romantic time that he had vowed he would never visit there again without me. I spent three days sleeping on my sofa, rather than going to bed, torn by the anxiety of not knowing for sure, terrified of possible loss. Jim had indeed found someone else in Hawai'i—he claimed, because he missed me too much!

During that period I suffered anxiety attacks in which I breathed rapidly and yet felt like I was suffocating, requiring me to breathe into a paper bag to return to a normal breathing pattern. I had never before had such attacks, and have not had them since. I believed I would recover from my grief without professional help— my friends and family were very good to me, and as I said, I knew the routine of a relationship's end. But I also was aware that without professional help I might not discern why this loss was so great.

I chose a therapist who was also a minister, because I didn't view this death of a relationship as merely having psychological implications, but spiritual as well. The therapeutic process refined the earlier insight as to my separation anxiety. I had been spending most of my free time at Jim's apartment, and my own apartment no longer felt like home. What's more, Jim's home, our nest, had been the one place where I had felt safe. I lived and worked in a society and a religious tradition that did not welcome me as gay, and in a congregation who welcomed me as gay, but whose love was understandably largely conditional on my job performance. I was hungry for the idealized home, not only "where they have to take you in," but they *want* to take you in, where you can kick back, put your feet up, and be comfortable. That's what Jim had become for me. Just when I felt safe, the proverbial rug had been taken out from under me. What I learned with a counselor's help was how important home was to me, a safe place, a sanctuary, whether within a spiritual community or within someone's arms. My second book had to do with this spiritual insight, *Come Home!*, which was all about the spirituality of homemaking.

In our relationship, I had mistakenly told Jim that I wanted to be a writer. I say mistakenly because of how unfairly he used my dream. In his previous relationship his partner kept saying he "wanted" to be something. Jim had grown impatient, and told him just to "be" what he wanted to be, instead of always wishing for it. As a way of distancing himself from me, Jim gave me the same parting advice, wanting to justify his ending our relationship by imagining I was like the previous partner. I became defensive, but I didn't need to be. I had never been accused of being an underachiever. The second half of my "mistake" in sharing my dream of being a writer with Jim was that I already *was* a writer!

Words have been vital for me from my earliest memory, whether spoken or written. This was my means to grasp what I otherwise could not grasp, to assert a little control of things over which I seemed to have no control. Putting things in words helped and helps me decipher my own take on reality. It is my yoga, my spiritual practice, my place of integrity, my home. And so I had chosen both a profession and a cause which required writing: ministry was my profession, an inclusive church my cause. I wrote weekly sermons and monthly columns, as well as the occasional article or speech. Giving myself fully over to writing seemed a fantasy and surely meant poverty.

Two deaths forced me to reconsider my reservations about focusing on writing. George Salerno was married to a member of my congregation, Cindy Ames. Both were in theater, keeping separate living quarters in New York City and West Hollywood. My first conversation with George occurred when Cindy handed me the church phone one Sunday, having rung him up in his room at a V.A. hospital in New York where he was being treated for a chronic illness. He came West and continued his treatment and occasional hospitalizations at the V.A. hospital in Westwood. There

I visited him, not merely out of vocational obligation, but because I found our conversations intriguing. Proximity to death made him wax philosophical. Once he told me that death was to him like the edge of, say, this table, and he would demonstrably caress the edge of the rollaway table that hovered over his lap as he sat up on his hospital bed. What he meant was that both were certainly there, but a matter of indifference. There was something calming in his presence, something calming too as I considered my own death. He was well-read, quoting people like George Santayana as if they had been chums, and he had a way with words that another writer could appreciate.

George had written, but, according to him, not enough. And he had never published anything major. And then he died, as much as hospital authorities would permit, for they felt compelled to resuscitate him, and what survived on the machines for a few days was not George Salerno. Once again, death was associated with some kind of failure, this time, the misperceived "failure" of medical staff. "We have to fix this," they may have told themselves. If only our society could accept death with George's equanimity—recognizing its inevitable presence, as the edge of a table—medical staff might have had permission to step back and take a breath even as George let go his last. Release, Death encourages, relax. In fairness, unless there is a "do not resuscitate" order from the patient or a patient's power of attorney, hospital staff are duty-bound to do what they can, lest a malpractice lawsuit is handed them. George's wife was also faced with an unfair dilemma: should she "pull the plug," by taking him off the machines? With his mother hovering protectively, she chose not to do so. Blessedly George left us on his own. Our drama was not his drama.

Tommy Thompson was quite a different type of writer. His novelized versions of real life murder mysteries rode high on the *New York Times* bestseller lists. He wrote me a brief handwritten note after seeing me on television during the 1978 San Diego General Assembly of the Presbyterian Church. We had been defeated on the controversial issue of gay ordination. "You and your colleagues may have thought you lost," Tommy wrote, "but you actually won." His implication was that our efforts, covered by the media, had awakened the public consciousness to our cause. He added that he noticed we lived in the same zip code, and invited me to give him a call and come by for a drink sometime. By the time we were able to arrange that meeting in his spacious and well-appointed Hollywood

Hills home, I was at work on another project, an interfaith service to give witness to religious opposition to the anti-gay Briggs initiative on the California ballot that fall. I had just contacted the Greek Theater, an outdoor amphitheater in L.A.'s Griffith Park, for rental rates. Tommy asked me how much it would cost to rent the theater. I told him. He said, "Let me do that." He had wanted to contribute to the "No on 6" campaign, but donors' names were listed in the public record. Instead, he could make the donation privately to my church. In these more tolerant times, it's difficult to remember that even our allies were afraid of being publicly associated with gay rights. Tommy wasn't afraid for himself, but for his two teenage sons, who might get taunted in school: after all, the initiative was to fire gay teachers and any teachers who supported gay rights.

I was grateful for his support in this cause, but even more grateful for his encouragement of me as a writer. "How did you start writing books?" I asked. Tommy, with matter-of-fact Texan charm, chuckled as he said, "Because I lost my job!" When *Life Magazine* folded, he explained, it closed the Paris office, which I believe he managed. He started researching prominent and recent crimes and writing them as novels, a genre which I never read until I met him. He had become, in the process, not only a successful writer, but a celebrity, yet one bemused by such fame. His final book, the novel *Celebrity*, his first attempt at pure fiction, explored the many dimensions of that mixed "blessing" and, he felt, uniquely American phenomenon.

I once found Tommy wearing a t-shirt that read "Semi-Celebrity" on the front. Smiling, I asked him about it, and he told me the story of being taken off a flight before departing New York because flight attendants confused him with another passenger, an obnoxious drunk, that Tommy's gentlemanly way would not allow him to tattle on. But once inside the airport again, Tommy decided to use whatever clout he had to have the mistake rectified. Explaining to me that he *never* did this sort of thing, he nonetheless pulled out that day's *New York Times*, opening it to a full-page ad for his new book, and said, "That's me. I was in New York doing the *Today Show* this morning to promote the book." The jaded agent phoned the airline's public relations department, telling them, "We have a semi-celebrity that has been off-loaded from our morning flight to Los Angeles." Now humorously recounting the anecdote to me, he turned around so I could see the words on the back of the "Semi-Celebrity" t-shirt: "Off-load at will." One of his friends had had the shirt specially made after hearing the story. Always concerned about even minor injustices, I asked what had been done to make it right, only to discover the airline had simply put him on the next flight. He had mentioned the incident to a relative who was a lawyer, but had been discouraged from pursuing legal action. "Even the pope could go into court with a legitimate lawsuit, and come out looking dirty," the relative had explained. No wonder celebrities don't sue more often!

It was that very celebrity status that intimidated me in our friendship. On one occasion, for example, he introduced me to several movie stars during a screening party at a movie studio, including one of my idols, Vincent Price. I wasn't sure of my worthiness, and I don't think I recognized how willing Tommy was to be friends. Tommy took me out to his Malibu house one weekend, and encouraged me to make use of it as I wished whenever it was free. Once when I was there alone, I took a phone message from Robert Wagner's secretary reminding Tommy of "Bob's" 50th (as I recall) birthday party. Tommy was good friends with Wagner and his wife, Natalie Wood. When she drowned off a boat near Catalina Island, it was Tommy who was quoted on television: "We all have a fragile grip on life," he said, putting it in context. At the time I wrote him a note commending the way he responded, mentioning the effects a celebrity's death has on all of us, and he pleased me by saying he would show it to "Bob" after awhile. This was heady stuff for me.

I was also bent on not taking advantage of his offer of the Malibu house. I did use it on several weekends, but not as much as I could have. Nor did I spend time in his company as much as I think he desired. Admittedly this was due, in part, to his way of carrying on a conversation, constantly asking questions—the indefatigable journalist in his blood. He and a screenwriter and I saw the film *The Black Stallion* together, about a boy and a horse on an island. I relished the film's cinematography. But afterward, over dinner at the elegant Winter Garden Chinese restaurant (where I once dined with Carter Courtney as his "thank you" for my support), Tommy and his friend went on and on about how bad the screenplay was. It occurred to me later that their critique may really have been about the fact that there was so little dialogue. These men lived on and for words, and their appetite was not sated by so much silence.

One evening, Tommy and I watched the first episode of the sequel series to *Roots*. Tommy was working on *Serpentine*, a book about a handsome young Eurasian man who befriended tourists overseas only to murder and rob them. The following evening, I watched the second episode of *Roots* with a new friend named York, a photographer. During commercials York told me about his cousin who disappeared while traveling abroad. Eventually it was discovered that his cousin had fallen victim to a charming man posing as a tour guide. "In fact, some guy's writing a book about it," York said, and I was stunned by the coincidence, explaining that I had just had dinner with the "guy" the night before! York's cousin was one of three women Tommy profiled at length in the beginning of the book. Later, though the film director "Billy" Freidkin bought the rights, he never made the movie because a copycat writer (the liability of writing true stories) got his book made into a movie first.

I tell the story because I am often left in wonder at how life—I can't help but make the connection, forgive me—"serpentinely" twists in and out of our experiential nooks and crannies, and how, at the same time, Death may bring together disparate people. Synchronicity, Jung called it, the meaningful coincidence; though, in this instance, I am not sure of the meaning. I do know that I am continually finding meaning in events that others might find meaningless. As I grow older, I have more and more experiences of synchronicity. Death could be considered one of those meaningless events, I know. Given that I write to "manage" events over which I have little control, it's small wonder that I would write this book, gleaning meaning from deaths I have experienced.

My parents were the ones to call and tell me of Tommy's death, which they heard on the news. I was at my church office and went out and bought a newspaper to read the scant information provided. Liver cancer, diagnosed just a month earlier, was listed as the cause. Tommy was only forty-nine years of age. I remembered that, to encourage me getting health insurance, he had told the story of his picking up something when he was doing research for *Serpentine* in India, where the water supply was not always well separated from the sewer system. It had cost $20,000 to diagnose. I wondered whether that had something to do with his death.

I had not seen him much in the final year of his life. The most recent visit, however, was very significant. He was on a spiritual quest, tapping into his feelings through various means, including hypnosis, which helped him remember events from his youth in Texas that added an authentic backdrop to the beginning of *Celebrity*. Over dinner he told me about an extremely meaningful weekend retreat in which he had "cried like a baby"—and Tommy was not given to such displays. Either he had a premonition or a secret diagnosis that prompted him to face issues of life and death. I attended his memorial service at nearby Beverly Hills Presbyterian Church, and Dinah Shore spoke for many of his friends when she expressed regret he had kept to himself his final month of life. But Tommy had told her in a phone call, "Everything I've wanted to do in life, I've done twice." Typical of him to say something witty and comforting to console his friends. I was "down" after the service, not only because a friend's life was cut short, a life promising so many more writings. I felt sad because I had shortchanged my own life by not fully pursuing the friendship.

Taken together, the deaths of George and Tommy prompted my decision to go half time in my work at the church so I could have more time to write, and, three years later, to abandon work at my church altogether. George's "failure" as a writer was as much an instigator for me as Tommy's success. Tommy, trying to encourage me, had once asked what my writing discipline was. His was writing 8 a.m. to noon, ten pages per day, every day, even on vacation. His friends knew never to call during that time, though I learned this the hard way: he was friendly but brusque at my interruptive morning phone call. The afternoons he devoted to business, talks, teaching at a prison, and tennis. Evenings were for socializing or the arts. When he asked the question about my own writing discipline, he quickly answered it himself, "Oh, but you're working all day. It's hard to make the time you need, probably."

Today I believe that the principal block to anyone becoming a writer is discipline. So I imitated Tommy's, though I could seldom write ten pages in four hours, so I extended my writing into the afternoon. At times, to make deadlines, I have written as much as fifteen hours per day. Like Tommy, I feel content with a day only if I've been writing. Death has taught me discipline, a word that for me has connotations of boundaries and focus and mindfulness rather than punishment. Death also taught me to take risks, such as leaving my job. I have never been financially secure, let alone anywhere near as financially successful as Tommy. But I have been spiritually satisfied—even, I might say, spiritually wealthy. Most people need a brush with their own deaths to transform their lives. By extrapolation, George and Tommy's deaths provided a brush with my own mortality—rather, finiteness. I only have so many days. How do I want to spend them? To turn Joseph Campbell's spiritual advice into a question, what bliss do I want to follow? *The New York Times* recently reported studies revealing that we procrastinate over pleasurable, not just unpleasant, activities—whether using airline mileage, gift cards, or taking vacations—thinking there'll be plenty of time "later on" to enjoy them. Death reminds me that "later on" is not guaranteed.

Today I believe my fear of death has more to do with missing out on life in the moment, death in its many everyday forms of wasting time in unfulfilling activity, a foreshadowing of being boxed up for all time. Death adds an eschatological theme to my life. Eschatology is about "end times," the Day of Judgment or the end of the age of Jewish prophets, the *parousia* (return of Christ) in Christianity. Life is, in this sense, lived backwards, as present deeds will be evaluated by some form of Final Judgment, yours, others, or God's. The film *Memento* does a remarkable job depicting this cinematographically, as the film begins with the ending, and tells the story by going back in time, segment by segment, because the protagonist has no short-term memory and must rely on tattoos and memos to warn himself of dangers from the past and remind himself who he is, or who he thinks he is.

Death, to me, is personalized eschatology. There is an advantage imagining the end of life to appreciate its origin and present. I know cultures and religions other than my own enjoy an understanding of time, and thus life, as cyclical, and I am partly convinced. But there is an impetus that comes from the linear time of our Western tradition that is advantageous in realizing we're not going to pass this way again, that this is the time to do what we please, and I mean please as in the deepest sense of pleasure. Many things we regard as pleasure are mere distractions, escapes from life. Henri Nouwen warned about living our lives as entertainment, a word whose etymology literally means "to keep between." Lest my emphasis on personal fulfillment seem selfish or self-absorbed, I quickly add that I subscribe to Frederick Buechner's notion that true vocation is "the place where your deep gladness meets the world's deep need." Another recent study of how our brains perceive time indicates that we more readily remember time when doing or experiencing meaningful activities.

My preference is to think of time as a cross between cyclical and linear, a spiral. Yes, there are seasons of our lives, and I don't mean just four seasons between youth and age. I mean we live through multiple changes of season: one season we let go, another we create, another we preserve, another we rest. Then we go through the cycle all over again.

Death can never be taken alone as transforming. Death, I believe, can only be transformative if it punctuates life. The early Christian teachers (known historically as the "church fathers") would be somewhat at odds with fundamentalists who merely claim, "Christ died to atone for your sins." Early church writers and teachers affirmed that the life, death, and resurrection of Christ—all three—brought atonement, at-one-ment with God. They did not single out the crucifixion as salvific alone. That emphasis came later in church history, during a time of plague, famine, and war. People began to see their own suffering upon the cross, and it captured their spiritual imagination, to the detriment of a larger picture. There has to be life on either side of death for there to be transformation. The deaths of George and Tommy were meaningful to me because their lives touched mine and transformed its future. Their lives and deaths brought atonement, at-one-ment, with my self as a writer. However they may live on in God's eternal realms, they live on in me. Movies and books are often considered "realistic" if they have no Hollywood or fairy tale happy ending. Yet, just as my first book did not reflect my whole reality because it initially ended with a crucifixion, as my friend Scott Rogo pointed out to me, so even horrible endings do not reflect the full reality that life goes on, at the very least enough life to reflect on the meaning of unhappy endings.

In the Greek of Christian scriptures, there is an aorist tense of verbs which suggest a past action having present effects. That's how the life, death, and resurrection of Jesus were understood by his followers. And that's how I understand the role death plays in my life: a past action having present effects. The quality of my life is related to how much death I have experienced, in the sense of absorbed. Putting these words on paper is Death's direct effect on me. For an artist, it might be a brush stroke. For a chef, it might be seasoning. For a janitor, it might be polish. For an accountant, it might be totals. Care and fulfillment in every field of endeavor may come from mindfulness of life's passing quality.

How much more so in the spiritual enterprise! Every path is spiritual, but some more self-consciously than others. And, when combined with writing, a spiritual writer's words become the bread crumbs to follow into the contemplative forest. Henri Nouwen was the author of more than forty books on the spiritual life. Ordained a Roman Catholic priest in Holland in 1957, Nouwen traveled to the United States to study religion and psychology at the famed Menninger Clinic in Topeka, Kansas. He then taught in the psychology department of Notre Dame. He returned to Holland to teach and obtain a doctorate in theology. Invited to teach psychology and religion at Yale Divinity School, he agreed to do so on the condition that he teach spirituality. He had come to realize that psychology and religion found their integrity in the spiritual life. His peripatetic pilgrimage included two six-month stints with the Trappists at the Abbey of the Genesee in upstate New York, a six-month stay in Bolivia and Peru, and teaching at Harvard. Finally he came to "rest" in L'Arche, an international community centered on people with mental disabilities, initially in France, and the final decade of his life, in Toronto.

Henri was first my professor, then my friend. Along with hundreds of others, I studied with Henri at Yale in the 1970's. We became friends, but like my friendship with Tommy Thompson, his status, first, as a professor, and subsequently, his celebrity as a renowned spiritual writer, sometimes kept me at an awe-filled distance—my problem, not his. Henri welcomed and sometimes expected intimacy, and our visits and correspondence, while limited, always cut to the heart of our identities and our relationships. Just as Tommy's journalistic interrogations could be off-putting, Henri's expectations of intense conversation could feel demanding. Yet the old adage proved true: when you need a teacher, one will come. By the time I came to seminary I was less interested in theology than I was in the spiritual life. At the time, Yale Divinity School, with Henri as catalyst, was fertile soil for cultivating "the inner voice of love," a title Henri gave to one of his most personal journals.

So when a member of his community in Toronto phoned to tell me of his unanticipated death so that I "would not first hear of it through the media," the simultaneous and sudden clap of thunder that literally shook my house as I held the phone paralleled the shock of the news of the heart attack that claimed Henri's life. Both presaged the start of a storm, gusts and downpour outside, heaves and tears inside. Henri would have loved the synchronicity. I had not experienced such grief since the death of my father. I realized that Henri had been a spiritual father to me, and it was not until his death that I began to identify him to others as my mentor in things spiritual. Death revealed to me the depth of our relationship.

I struggled with the decision to attend his funeral mass in Toronto. Having joined the downwardly mobile as a writer meant that rarely could I attend important events in the lives of my friends at a distance, for lack of funds. Then it occurred to me I had enough award mileage to cash in for the trip, and I am very grateful I did. Brad Colby, who had phoned me with the news, met me at the airport and took me to stay with him. His L'Arche household "adopted" me for my visit, and I was included in all the public and private vigils, the funeral mass, and the relatively private burial. Henri keenly believed in the visible presence of the body for such farewells, so the wooden casket, made in the "Woodery" by members of the community, was always open for viewing, touching, and inserting sacramentals of photographs and other mementoes. In the vestibule of the unfinished Slavic cathedral in Richmond Hill, Ontario, Henri "greeted" his mourners before the coffin was closed for the procession into the heart of the church.

Beneath glowing clouds, whose shadowy edges dripped occasional rain, the largest cast bell in Canada rung out the beginning of the service. I looked around at those gathered and realized that most were from groups many spiritual communities fail to include adequately or equitably, the "least of these": women, children, the poor, people with disabilities, the divorced, gays and lesbians, artists, more recent immigrants, native peoples, people of color, those of other faiths, and people with AIDS. The metaphor of the unfinished cathedral that housed us became evident as I recognized that Henri had gathered around himself in life and now in death the very people his own spiritual guide, Jesus, would have welcomed to his table. Like Jesus, Henri had made his "home" with us, a metaphor for the spiritual life that he had embraced just as I had. He had written in *The Inner Voice of Love* about bringing his body "home," that is, accepting his body in his spirituality, with all of its needs and desires, vulnerabilities and limitations. At the vigil for his community, the hall was decorated with signs saying things like, "Welcome Home, Henri!" At first I thought these were drawn in honor of a life well-lived; then I realized these were signs left hanging from his homecoming a few weeks earlier after a year sabbatical. If one has to die, I thought, what better time than as one is returning from sabbatical! Additional irony lay in the fact that he died in his homeland of Holland, en route to St. Petersburg to do a film documentary about a painting of homecoming in the

Hermitage museum: Rembrandt's "Return of the Prodigal." Henri had written a book about the painting, confessing his own desire to be welcomed home as well as his own "fatherly" vocation to welcome others home. The theme for his funeral mass was "Coming Home."

During the burial at the cemetery, a family member described Henri as a child always reaching out to be picked up and held. Then each of us took part in the old tradition of spilling a shovel full of earth into the grave. The first shovels of soil from family members made thunderous sounds as they landed atop the wooden lid of the casket. As each of the friends took our turn, the sound became muted with the added dirt. When my turn came, I sprinkled the earth gently from my shovel, wanting a softer goodbye.

Henri once described his Uncle Anton's burial. His Uncle "Toon" had been the priest of the earlier generation of the family, one who had been well known in the ecumenical movement in Europe. In a Toronto diner, Henri and I had been talking about the challenge of celibacy, especially for one like Henri who so desired intimacy. He told me that grief was expressed at his uncle's death, but then everyone left the graveside to socialize together. "Nobody mourned him as if their very lives depended on it," he said. Poignantly, Henri looked me in the eye and said, "I would like to have somebody at my grave whose life is radically altered by my death." At the time I gave him a rather obvious and too facile response, telling him thousands of lives would have their lives radically altered by his death—meaning his readers—but that was not the comfort he sought.

I can testify personally as one who was radically altered by Henri's death. I am also certain I am not alone. As my plane lifted above a rain-swept Toronto the day following his funeral mass, I felt Henri in my heart, and I knew he was not gone, and I knew I was stronger. "Trust the Spirit more," he had once challenged me regarding my detailed preparations for speaking engagements. Somehow, having said goodbye to Henri, I felt more confident in myself, in my ability to speak from the heart, to be a spiritual guide myself. Perhaps this is an experience akin to what followers of other spiritual leaders have enjoyed, realizing their mentors never really leave them, thus having experiences of resurrection, voices, visions, or other manifestations of their teachers' presence. In the mystical Gospel of John, Mary's first word upon recognizing her risen Christ was "Teacher." One who is truly holy, sacred, and spiritual can never be buried, either by dirt or dogma. Neither can one who is loving and beloved, which, I sense, is the same thing as holiness.

Neal Douglas Klotz speaks of the ancient Hebrew concept of time. Nomadic, travelling in caravans, they viewed themselves following those who had gone before them. Thus their ancestors were not "dead" to them, just ahead of them in the caravan, leading their way. I like this. Henri and others who have passed from life still lead me, still shape me, still influence me. Though I will write of my parents' deaths in a later chapter, I realize I am still learning from them decades later. Something will happen and I will think, "That's what Mom meant!" or "That's what Dad felt!" As well, Henri continued to be my teacher and friend, leading me into new teaching relationships and new friendships.

My profound grief over Henri's death prompted me to write and speak and lead retreats on his life and writings. The media's almost total failure to note Henri's passing prompted me to write an Op-Ed piece for *The Atlanta Journal Constitution*. Three women called me as a result of reading the piece. One was crying to learn for the first time of Henri's death, explaining to me that she and her pastor-husband read Henri's words to each other as they drove on vacations. Another called to invite me to speak on Henri's understanding of community to her Catholic laywomen's circle. The third called to say, having left the Catholic Church long ago, that she was thrilled to hear of a priest like Henri, and wanted to know the names of some of his books. In one of his last books, *Our Greatest Gift*, Henri had written of how much of the "fruitfulness" of our lives can only be harvested after our brief life spans.

Many spiritual people, me included, rely on sacred texts for inspiration. But not all sacred texts are written documents from ancient times. Our lives themselves are sacred texts. Henri consulted his regularly for spiritual insight, one of the reasons his writings are so accessible. I have done the same. As the earlier deaths of two writer friends prompted me to create room in my life to write, so Henri Nouwen's death confirmed the need to consult not only the life experience of others, but also, my own life experience in my spiritual quest. In the words of the Quaker saying, "Let your life speak." Death may be terrifying and painful, and an occasion for grief. But it may also be an occasion for gratitude, an opportunity for comfort and pleasure. A paradox, to be sure; but the spiritual life thrives on paradox.

The mischievous joke at Henri's funeral was that his death was one "life experience" he would not get to write about. In truth, I believe he wrote about it in every one of his books. When I wrote my own book about Henri, I chose a blend of memoir and meditation. *Henri's Mantle: 100 Meditations on Nouwen's Legacy* demonstrated the integrity or sought-for integrity of Henri's words and deeds. Just as the prophet Elijah passed on his spiritual mantle to Elisha, so Henri gave his readers more than forty books on the spiritual life. I am blessed to be among them. And I too wish to pass on a mantle of hopeful words, a legacy that may inspire readers to live deeply in the face of death.

Chapter Five

Death by One's Own Hand

Often I impose a deadline on myself to be sure that something is written or achieved before the actual deadline, knowing how often variables can come into play and interfere with the completion of a task by a given time. Suicide is a self-imposed deadline, but not one that is friendly toward accomplishing anything but one's own demise—unless the intent is to take down others at the same time and avoid retribution. Suicide is more often a declaration, such as, "I can't do this!" or "I can't finish this!" or "I can't stand this anymore." Rarely does suicide serve as a prompt to accomplish; more often it serves to excuse someone from a burden perceived as too great to bear.

Suicide can be subtle or dramatic. I believe our culture prefers the subtler forms, possibly because it still gives us something to gossip about—whether to each other or through tabloid journalism—while distancing ourselves from blame. I have multiple acquaintances and a few friends of whom it could be said: He drank himself to death. She starved herself to death. She accidentally overdosed. He never got a handle on his obesity. She just didn't take care of herself. He wouldn't get checked regularly.

She drove recklessly. He hung out with the wrong crowd. He went off his medication. She just couldn't stop smoking. His behavior was risky. She couldn't stick with the program. She just wanted to die. And so on.

I fear stupid death. I don't want to die because of something I could have avoided or prevented. I don't like wasting *anything*, especially my life. I don't like to see others wasting anything either. If I don't appreciate something, it's usually because I feel the money or effort or talent or time it required could've been better spent. In other words, I value the sacrifice of the giver *more*, not less, because I value their resources and hate to see them squandered.

This attitude creates a paradox when seeking medical care. I inherited a blend of my mother's suspicion of the medical field and my father's cautious concern for his health. For most of my life I was able to say my mother hadn't seen a doctor, except when taking us kids, since the day I was born. My father, on the other hand, would go to the doctor more often than any of us. How that plays out for me is that I at least try to get a physical exam annually. My fear of losing my life prematurely or unnecessarily trumps my fear of wasting money on doctors and medical tests. I also take care of my body, watching what I eat and exercising regularly. When I experimented with drugs as a young man, or even now as I enjoy my wine, my fear of losing valuable time or my life kept and keeps me in check to prevent excess.

But all this is not to say I didn't contemplate suicide. In the raging surge of adolescent hormones and the self-discovery of my homosexuality in an extremely anti-gay world, I pondered the dramatic rejection of the life fate had dealt me. Life could be lonely and painful, and I suffered a lot before I could accept myself. But death by my own hand was also, for me, to send a message, and ultimately, words and writing gave me another and less devastating way to deliver that message. As a kind of "victim" of others' suicides, I began to realize what a terrible slap in the face it is to those who love you, as if they have failed you miserably. I once led a memorial service for someone who killed himself by setting his apartment on fire, dying an agonizing death as a burn victim three days later. During a time of reflections in the service, his friends spoke not only of their grief but also of their anger at all his drama and their pain as fellow 12-steppers that he could not accept their love and their help.

Yet there are some whose depression or grief or condition is so grave or painful that they should not be judged for wanting to bring an end to it. Assisted suicide should be an option, but the problem is where to draw the line—when should it be allowed and when should it be discouraged? I had a friend infected with HIV who chose to end his life rather than become sick with AIDS in the days before much could be done about the virus. It struck me as odd, because he was a fundamentalist Christian who had an obsession with images of the end-times, the mark of the beast, the number 666, and the anticipated tribulation. Given his paranoia about God's eternal punishment, I wondered how he could possibly justify taking his own life. Though he no doubt experienced emotional pain and religious shame testing positive, contrast his as yet physically painless experience of HIV with another friend who, after years of suffering the various opportunistic infections, wasting syndrome, and fatigue associated with AIDS, and losing most of his friends to the disease, set aside enough pills to end his life with dignity in the arms of his lover. The latter friend's course feels more appropriate than the former.

In seminary my counseling class took a field trip to a local mortuary. As we stood in the room where bodies were prepared, many of us (we later learned) were hoping the mortician would unveil the body that lay beneath a white sheet before us on a slab, so intrigued were we by its unapologetic presence. Instead he made a strangely defensive remark about how many suicides he had taken off "seminary hill," as if he feared we were somehow judging his profession as we glanced around at the tools of his trade.

And indeed, he may have been called to my dormitory my first semester, if a resident had not survived an overdose of pills. But he was not a seminarian; rather, he was a student at another of Yale's graduate schools. He lived in our dorm because of a surplus of rooms at the divinity school and a shortage elsewhere. He was short on social skills. I did not know him well, but he had once asked to borrow my typewriter. On that occasion, I suddenly realized what a personal request this was—an "aha" for me regarding my attachment to my basic writing instrument, like Lord Byron's attachment to his quill as an extension of himself. I mentioned this to another dormmate, explaining, "It was as if he had asked to borrow my underwear." The dormmate said that in fact the student *had* borrowed *his* underwear!

He was not well-liked, and it took several days before anyone missed him and knocked on his door, rousing him from a sleep of three days. He was taken to the hospital, where we, as dutiful would-be pastors, visited him, and where he mercilessly made fun of the person in the next bed for being there for "twisted balls." Even so, I felt the requisite guilt for not liking him—after all, I was a Christian training for ministry—and I self-righteously took exception when two friends back at the dorm debated whether it was a *serious* suicide attempt. One of them, it turned out, had considerably more experience with suicide than I did, as his college roommate had attempted suicide, and he had literally carried him in his arms to the college medical facility. My expressed dismay at their cynicism was possibly a way to take the high ground in his defense to absolve my own guilt.

The most spectacular suicide in my personal and professional history I experienced indirectly, after the fact—but then, that's usually the way suicide presents itself. The 1960s and 1970s were a high time of drugs and drama among American college youth. The pastor with whom I worked in my first position after seminary, the Rev. Dr. Ross Greek, had opened the doors of the West Hollywood Presbyterian Church to the flower children that congregated on the nearby Sunset Strip, a stretch of Sunset Boulevard unincorporated by the City of Los Angeles and governed by Los Angeles County. The area proved to be a more lenient atmosphere for L.A.'s equivalent of San Francisco's hippies to grow, with their clubs, coffee houses, and other hangouts— sometimes outdoor public spaces.

Ross was known as the "Chaplain to the Strip," and our small facilities, with the help of volunteers from other churches, provided food, showers, and shelter for the homeless runaways and castaways that came to the area hoping "to find themselves," free from family and hometown restraints. Ross led daily "rap sessions" in the fellowship hall and established off-site halfway homes for ex-addicts, ex-offenders, and those with mental disabilities. Pews were rearranged in a diamond shape to permit a kind of worship-in-the-round in the chapel-sized sanctuary, proving hospitable to creative worship that included guitar music, dance (thanks to Marge and Gower Champion who were participants in the church), and drama (thanks to acting coach Ned Mandarino, author of *The Transpersonal Actor*). The sound system had been donated when Tim Rice and Andrew Lloyd Weber premiered the first recording of *Jesus Christ Superstar* to record executives and distributors in the sanctuary. The bars on the windows of the fellowship hall were not to deter criminals, but rather, to keep police out, who were allegedly interested in the records kept by the L. A. Free Clinic that originated there, and who many believed were capable of planting pot on the premises to give an excuse for the occasional raid.

This was the grand and glorious past of the church that called me in 1977 to lead another Ross-inspired innovative ministry, this time within the gay community. The congregation had dwindled to twelve or less worshipers, but it still provided shelter for two homeless young men, one of whom resided in the fellowship hall building and the other in the separate sanctuary building. When I pointed out to Ross that we could save on utilities if they lived in the same building, he explained matter-of-factly, "Well, they don't get along." The halfway houses had evolved into independent entities, save one, which soon closed. And Ross, with a Ph.D. in psychology, continued to counsel the occasional lost youth that wandered in our doors or to visit with the flower children alums who might stop by to thank Ross for his help in the past.

One of the latter, whom I will call Nathan, visited Ross from time to time when experiencing enormous anxiety about an earlier deed. High on psychedelics, he hallucinated that the devil had possessed his kid sister and shot her in a fatal exorcism. It reveals Ross' influence with the court system that he persuaded the judge to eventually release Nathan into his care rather than incarcerate him for a longer period of time, for which Nathan's family, who lived in an exclusive beach community, was grateful. I met Nathan a couple of times, and he seemed a gentle, even diminutive man incapable of such violence—and surely one who had "learned his lesson."

I was out of town for a meeting of a national Presbyterian task force on which I served and Ross was purchasing church supplies at Smart & Final when Nathan stopped by the church one day, apparently distraught, according to witnesses, and no doubt extremely disturbed to find his pastor/therapist unavailable. The Denny's that then stood across the street had already witnessed more than its share of drama on Sunset Boulevard, including a long-haired and shoe-less young hippie who, when denied entrance to the restaurant, crossed the street and uprooted the church's wooden cross and lodged it in the coffee shop's doorway in protest.

This day, however, diners would witness the ultimate demonstration on the sidewalk that fronted the church as Nathan doused himself with flammable liquid and ignited it, a horrific suicidal conflagration reminiscent of Vietnamese Buddhist monks protesting war. Of course his war was with himself, and this served as an example of how suicides cannot all be judged by the same measure. Every time he chose life, he won a battle with his soul-wracking guilt. But in choosing death, he ended the war.

Of course, this made the news in a big and negative way—happening as it did the same week that an article about my own controversial work within the gay community appeared unbeknownst to me in *The Los Angeles Times*. Upon my return from New York, Ross Greek was in a rage, as if it were somehow my fault, possibly his displaced guilt. Strangely, months later, I received a phone call from Nathan! I immediately thought of Scott Rogo's book on phone calls from the dead, and it took some minutes into the call before I realized I was speaking to Nathan Sr., not Nathan Jr. The tone and inflections of their speech patterns uncannily and unnervingly matched.

Nathan's personal war brings me back to subtler expressions of suicide, which may become avenues in the immediate "battle" to ameliorate guilt and, cumulatively, ways to end the war. Addictions, obsessions, compulsions, depression, and even lethargy, in a myriad of expressions, I believe, partly grow out of not feeling "good enough"—faulty, guilty, shamed, sinful, callous, flawed. Some look to a God to forgive such imperfections, but this is only helpful if one is thereby led to forgive one's self. God or a friend or a parent or a child or a spouse cannot supplant the spiritual practice of forgiving oneself—in some ways, we each are the ultimate "god" that needs to be pleaded with, persuaded, placated, and converted. Prayer and meditation and reflection may be the sanctuaries for such conversion. But true self-forgiveness requires first taking responsibility, and too many in our world shift blame, scapegoat, and make excuses—if only in our own minds. That's why penance is spiritually healthy, whether ritually in formulaic prayers or metaphorically in acts of charity. Penance is a way of saying "I have something to make up for." Nathan's suicide taught me that I must forgive myself; otherwise I would be paralyzed, stunted, shutdown. Forgiveness is not just about the past and present; it's also, for me, about the future. I must be ready to forgive my future mistakes, imperfections, and even wrongdoing as well, otherwise I would be unable to move, grow, and be open.

I greatly admired Tony. I again use a pseudonym because in telling both Nathan's and Tony's stories I am more aware than ever that we do not know what bears may be in anyone's cave. Suicide is such a taboo in our culture; I want to shield them both from ungracious judgment. By writing of how differently they took their lives, I neither want to diminish their characters nor claim certain knowledge that only they had of their life experience. Just as with other deaths in this book, I can only say for certain what I took from the experiences.

Tony was handsome and smart and kind and in love. But his deeply spiritual nature included a nagging sense of call to the priesthood that took him out of a long-term relationship and into an order to become a Roman Catholic priest. It was painful to watch him and his partner separate after seeming to be "a perfect couple," especially during a period of my life when I was not so "perfected." Many of us who knew them, largely through their activism in the church and beyond, talked among ourselves of our dismay, while concurrently wanting to honor Tony's religious vocation. He joined an intellectually rigorous order, going to Boston for studies and training as a novitiate before returning to Los Angeles to serve a large parish in suburban Los Angeles. I received an invitation to his ordination but was unable to attend because of a conflict with my own church work. Over the years I would hear of him and his work, how well regarded he was, but he was one of those friends we all have with whom we lose direct contact, busy with our own lives as they are with theirs. My move to Atlanta geographically distanced us as well.

Years later I was invited to attend a men's retreat led by the Franciscan Richard Rohr, and there I met a recruiter for Tony's order who was from Southern California. When I asked if he knew Tony, he bluntly said, "He's dead."

"What? How? What happened?" I was stunned.

"They don't know exactly what happened, but his body was found in a dumpster," I was told. And then he proceeded to tell me the story. Tony had been serving among the poorer populations of the city, and, of all things, had become addicted to crack cocaine. He went into rehab, but relapsed, and as I recall the story, went into rehab again. He apparently died of a drug-related cause, but how he came to be in the dumpster was anybody's guess.

All I could think of was this beautiful man I had known:

handsome, intelligent, compassionate, thoughtful, faithful, called to serve—ending up in a dumpster. It was almost beyond imagining. I knew how radically addictions can change people; I had witnessed that firsthand in friends and acquaintances. The most loving can become the most cruel; the most truthful can become masterfully deceitful; the generous and thoughtful can become selfish and self-absorbed; the honest can become thieves; the happy and careful and contented can become depressed and reckless and suicidal. But I had not seen Tony being transformed into such a person. I can only see him as he had been. Him as he had been, now in a stinking, slimy dumpster.

Despite the many causes of addiction, any one of which could've affected Tony, I could not help but think that how he ended up had a direct relationship to what he had been denied in pursuit of ministry. To this day, I associate my own drug experimentation with the closet in one form or another, losing myself in the euphoria of pot or LSD or mescaline which even then I considered a form of suicide, if only for the length of time required to recover from the drug of choice. Tony's religious vocation had prohibited an intimate companion that might have been able to gauge the telltale signs of drug use soon enough to be of help. But people become hopelessly addicted even in relationship. Still, the euphoria he experienced with drugs may have been a substitute for the euphoria he once experienced in lovemaking before celibacy was imposed by his church. Or maybe drugs were a way to escape the guilt, strictness, and harshness of his religion. I'll never know.

Just as Nathan's suicide spoke of the vital necessity to be self-forgiving, Tony's suicidal path served as a harsh reminder to avoid situations where I could not be myself, no matter how otherwise fulfilling. A job opportunity, a regular salary, a relationship, societal recognition, personal security—any of these very good things could prove hazardous to my spiritual health and well-being if they required me to give up who I am as a writer, a spiritual explorer, a minister, and a sensual and sexual being. *Each* and *all* of these identities have served as conduits to divinity, to God, to life itself. Denial of any of these thwarts life and for me would be suicidal.

Chapter Six
Death by Plague

A minister friend described to me a frustrating experience getting men in her HIV-positive support group to talk about their feelings. One was greatly grieved at the recent death of a bowling companion from AIDS. After "spilling his guts," sobbing and heaving, the first response from another member of the group was, "So where do you bowl?"

Similarly, my temptation is to go right to the lessons death by AIDS taught me, rather than rehearse a painful history. It has been said that many of us who have gone through the earlier years of the AIDS crisis carry a wound that we do not like to talk about, an overwhelming loss that we cannot "process"—whatever that means, and as if that were even possible. My uncles who fought in World War II did not like to talk about their battles either, though one had such horrible nightmares he refused to sleep in the same bed with his wife for fear he might kill her in his sleep. And with AIDS there's been no absolute peace treaty signed to give us "closure"—again, whatever the hell that means. I consider "closure" a pop-psychology invention clichéd by the media, one that may even guilt those who cannot achieve it. For true grief the only absolute closure

I'll experience is my own death. So, though tempted to begin with the present, that's not where my spiritual learning took place. It took place in the midst of disappointment, disillusionment, terror, suffering, and death by a contemporary plague.

The elation of the victory party in a ballroom of a Beverly Hills hotel after the defeat of Prop 6, the Briggs' initiative on the California ballot in 1978, reminded me of Psalm 126, "When God restored the fortunes of Zion, we were like those who dream. . . ." I felt a part of the exuberant joy in the hug Ivy Bottini and David Mixner, leaders of the "No on 6" campaign in Southern California, gave one another on stage when they announced the anti-gay schoolteacher initiative had been defeated. As part of the campaign, I had organized a major event at L.A.'s Greek Theater, an "Ecumenical Service for Human Rights," attended by 1500 people and featuring singers Odetta and Peter Yarrow, along with religious leaders opposing the pernicious initiative. The event got good press at a time when so many religious leaders "on the other side" promoted the discriminatory bill through the media and from their pulpits. Our successful campaign against the initiative served as a heady time for our community when we saw that victory over prejudice was possible.after a string of defeats from Florida to Oregon. Anything felt possible now.

That's why the first reported cases of AIDS—first known as "gay cancer" and then as "GRID"(Gay Related Immune Deficiency)"— in the years that followed somewhat, but not entirely, deflated my sense of possibility for the movement to which I had committed my life and my livelihood. At best, AIDS was a detour on our way to full civil rights; at worst, it served as "justification" for the continued denial of our rights. A most important lesson that death by AIDS taught an otherwise privileged white male like myself was how marginalized or "less valuable" people got ignored by mainstream society and its health care systems, whether they were gay men, racial minorities, the poor, women (especially lesbians), or people with disabilities. Political mobilization was necessary, else their health and social concerns would never gain the attention of the media and the powers that be. In the language of ACT-UP: silence really did equal death. "Do not go gentle into that good night," I earlier quoted the poet Dylan Thomas. But the next line of advice to his aging father, "Rage, rage against the dying of the light," especially rang true for gay men in their twenties and thirties.

The first person I knew to die of AIDS was a respected activist who had helped defeat the Briggs' initiative. The second was the owner of the copy shop that provided discounts for printing our church bulletins and newsletters. From these and other acquaintances, AIDS crept closer to colleagues and friends. The early mistaken notion that this was a disease of the "fast lane" of drug use and casual sex did not assuage my fear, as I had had enough sex to warrant anxiety. As I would write later, men with purer hearts than mine were succumbing to AIDS, sometimes literally dying "over the weekend" without prior diagnosis. Each death struck terror in my heart, as well as grief.

In 1984, I received notice that a friend, someone I dated while at Yale, had died unexpectedly. Bill Harwood had been named one of ten up-and-coming young conductors of the year. At the time of his death, he was in transition from serving as an associate conductor of the Houston Grand Opera (HGO) to the New York City Opera. He died in Arkansas, where he was also working with the Arkansas Symphony Orchestra. Bill and I had first noticed one another when he was helping to lead Easter worship in 1977 at Battel Chapel on the Yale University Campus. He was then conductor of the Yale Symphony Orchestra. When I subsequently met him at a bar, my opening line was, "What's a nice conductor like you doing in a place like this?"

I had the occasion to see three performances of HGO's revival of *Porgy and Bess*—twice in Los Angeles and then its opening performance at the Kennedy Center in Washington, D.C.—that Bill conducted while it toured the country. The last time I saw Bill was in 1982 when I was in Houston to attend the annual national gathering of my denomination, and he invited me and a friend to the final concert of the season and afterward to a celebratory full-course dinner with a large group of friends in a private dining room of a posh restaurant. At the time, he was coping with a wasting syndrome that a Southern doctor was treating with diet and exercise, possibly a sign of what was to come. He was sympathetic when I learned while there that a friend of mine had just been diagnosed with melanoma and might have to come to Houston for follow-up treatment. He offered his place as a home base for us, if the need arose. Shortly after, upon receiving the discrete notice of his death in the mail, I phoned the friends listed, who could only tell me that a virulent pneumonia had taken his life shortly after its diagnosis. I could easily surmise it was the pneumonia associated with AIDS.

The sacred versions of mementoes are sacramentals, items that carry a spiritual significance to the believer. For more than a decade following Bill's death, I took comfort carrying my glasses in a hard case that Bill had given me. It had been his, and inside it bore his name and former address at his parents' home in the South. Now, this had not been a "special" gift—it was more, "Oh, you can use this." But for me, the offhandedness of the gesture did not diminish the generosity it represented. It connected me to Bill every time I bothered to look at his name when I opened the case, and it usually prompted a fond smile. I never changed the name and address, nor added my own. When I left the case, along with my glasses, at a restaurant on a trip to visit family in Los Angeles, I was saddened. I called the restaurant and asked my brother to go by there to see if it had been found, but I think no one understood its significance to me. Whoever found it probably sent it "home" to the name and address inside, and the present occupants at that location were surely puzzled when it arrived.

I am surrounded by many such sacramentals in my home and office: the wooden chalice given me by my first Christian boyfriend who decades later died of AIDS, a colorful cross Henri Nouwen brought me from El Salvador, and a ceramic tile depicting a hummingbird that I gave my mother when she came to associate a visiting hummingbird with the spirit of my late father, later to be returned to me upon her own death. Friends have kidded me because I have also proudly worn dead men's shoes and clothing that were given to me by their spouses or partners. These are but a few of the mementoes, the sacramentals, that link me to people who have died, and they are comforting touchstones of our intersecting lives. I realized why my mother had so many things she could not give or throw away: "so-and-so" gave me this, "so-and-so" gave us that, your father loved this chair, your grandmother loved this book. Moreover, almost everything I have reminds me of a time or event of my life that has passed away—a recording that made me feel I could accomplish anything when I was young, a book I read that comforted me in a period of great loss and grief, even things I don't like or don't use that someone gave me as a reminder of a meaningful visit together.

What I learned was that Bill Harwood's eyeglass case served as a kind of time machine that could take me back before AIDS, reminding me of his youth, his talent, the twinkle in his eye, and the youthful excitement of vocational possibility we shared. I came to understand that my home contains a myriad of sacred objects that link me to a cloud of witnesses to life and love and even my former selves.

In 1987, I read again Robert Jay Lifton's analysis of Hiroshima survivors, and found in it helpful insights for my own experience of AIDS. I first outlined the connection between AIDS and Hiroshima in a sermon for the West Hollywood Presbyterian Church, where I served, and then in an article entitled "AIDS and A-Bomb Disease" for a magazine, *Christianity and Crisis*. From there, the article found its way into a special issue on AIDS of the *New England Journal for Public Policy* and a book, *The AIDS Epidemic: Private Rights and the Public Interest*. It's strange to "hear myself" as I read the article now, more than two decades later, describing myself as thirty-six, the then average age of death of a person with AIDS. My first book was about to be published, and I had some hope of a fruitful writing career, yet I chose not to be tested for AIDS antibodies because at the time there was nothing to be done medically, and it would not have changed my behavior, as I already tried to practice safer sex.

According to Lifton's analysis in *Death in Life: Survivors of Hiroshima*, Hiroshima survivors came to be seen as a tainted group because radiation damage could manifest at any time, long after the initial exposure, even in their children. They were associated forever with dying and death. Survivors' guilt caused them to see those killed in the initial blast as "pure," and no memorial could suffice to extol their virtues. At the same time many felt responsible for their own predicament, being part of a nation that had waged war. Many became lifelong peace activists as an act of atonement.

Not only did HIV and AIDS survivors come to be seen as a tainted group, the whole gay community was as well. Already pariahs for being homosexual, unapologetically sexual and resistant to gender expectations, now all gay people were also associated with other societal taboos: disease and death. The same bigotry that led to the Briggs' initiative possessed legislators to consider quarantining the infected in concentration camps. Honoring our fallen, or fighting for justice for them, never seemed adequate, as ACT-UP continually reminded us, though the AIDS Quilt eventually proved a colorful and moving solution to the first of those dilemmas. And, as with all sexually transmitted diseases, people living and dying with HIV and AIDS often felt guilt or shame for their illness. Survivors dedicated themselves professionally or as volunteers and donors to creating and supporting and working through numerous AIDS agencies to help those living with HIV, agitating for their rights and care, as well as encouraging safer sexual practices within our community and the broader society.

Lifton's analysis also highlighted various modes of immortality that were problematic for us. Too often, gay people were denied living on in their families' loving memories, denied the possibility of living on in children, separated from nature in urban environments, cut off from lasting accomplishments by early deaths, limited by illness and fatigue in celebrating life, and excommunicated from spiritual communities and their God. In such a vacuum, many created their own non-biological extended families, supported queer and questioning youth, enjoyed their pets and plants, worked feverishly to accomplish vocational goals, gave "fab-u-lous" dinners and parties, and created welcoming spiritual communities while discerning a more loving God or benevolent universe.

But this was not the case for all. I took the Midwestern mother of a person with AIDS, who was being treated at St. John's Hospital in Santa Monica, on my favorite walk in the nearby park that stretches along the palisades overlooking the Pacific Ocean. The walk gave her a breather from her and her husband's attentive but stressful care of their son Tim, virtually immobilized by the bloody sores of Kaposi's sarcoma and the wasting syndrome associated with AIDS. She asked me about my work with our shared denomination, and was dismayed to learn how unloving it was in its exclusive and judgmental policies. All the more poignant was that she and her husband knew God loved their son, but—despite that assurance—they could not persuade Tim that God loved him. The church had done its dirtiest work, instilling in him self-loathing for his sexuality and self-blame for his illness.

One evening while I was visiting Tim, the parents decided it was time to leave for the night. I wondered at this choice, as I felt the end was near, but they were exhausted. They encouraged me to leave as well, strangely, to attend a church fundraising outing at a gay "Superman Contest." As I watched beautiful and healthy men's bodies in swimsuits parade before us, all I could think of was Tim's emaciated body near death, and I realized there were no "men of steel" that could withstand as small a thing as a virus. I discovered the next morning that the parents were called back to the hospital that night for Tim's final moments. What I learned in that moment was that I had become experienced at gauging when death was near.

What prompted me to write the sermon and the subsequent article about Hiroshima and AIDS survivors was itself an attempt at transcendence, to forever link two disparate experiences of human survival and suffering. Wrapping such a painful experience in words gave me a sense of control that was an illusion. Whether words offered in prayer or words offering meaning, they served as a way of bringing order to chaos. One letter writer to *Christianity and Crisis* rebuked my "death-dripping sentiment" in angry denial of the import of AIDS on his life. As a friend who has survived AIDS for almost thirty years once told me, "Denial gets an unjustifiably bad rap. It can sometimes be healthy!"

Larry Patchen revealed to me a spiritual path independent of words. He worked in food services, as a manager, when what he particularly delighted in was hands-on food preparation. For our congregation's conferences, intended to reconcile people of different points of view, it was not the experts or authorities or shared knowledge that brought people together as much as Larry's meals. He taught many of us how to create a banquet for a large number of people quickly: mass food acquisition, washing, preparation, cooking, and serving. Though there were surely tense moments in our church's small kitchen, Larry's beaming face is what I remember as he successfully brought us together over tasty appetizers, delicious pastas, and refreshing desserts.

So when, after a long battle with AIDS, Larry called me to tell me he was ready to let go, it seemed a precious gift. He was used to control, managing things, whether in his work or in the kitchen. He had had me and my partner over for dinner not long before for which he chose the pairing of every dish with different wines to our mutual delight. And before that, he hosted an elegant birthday "picnic" dinner party for his friends at the Greek Theatre to hear the Pointer Sisters sing "Slow Hands." Now, as he was facing imminent death, he was ready to let go, to let his partner and his friends and his spiritual community care for him. In such a circumstance, I believe, letting go and allowing others to care for you is a form of ministry, even an act of hospitality.

I had no words with which to respond to Larry. I looked down at the sermon I was preparing for Pentecost, the observance of when the Holy Spirit empowered the first followers of Jesus to speak in the languages of strangers. It is the undoing of the Genesis story when Yahweh confused the languages of those arrogantly building the Tower of Babel to get into heaven on their own terms and by their own means—the ultimate parable regarding the human need for control. Yet the Spirit gave me no words for my friend Larry. I looked across the room to a stack of sermons I had earlier been filing, and recognized them as my own "Tower of Babel," my own attempt to wrap the spiritual experience into neat and tidy word packages.

For a long time I have known the importance of silence in the spiritual life. But now, facing life's end, I understood the power of silence over words in welcoming the gift Larry was giving me as he revealed this new direction in his spiritual path, his fresh spiritual insight of letting go. Makes me think of the wonderful phrase in a prayer from *The Book of Common Prayer*: "O Lord: support us all the day long, until the shadows lengthen and the evening comes, and the busy world is hushed, and the fever of life is over . . ."

Recently I attended a visitation at a funeral home for a young man to whose fiancé I was giving pastoral support. I had forgotten how much well-meaning but questionable theology is offered to survivors as I heard people give words of comfort in her loss. She was gracious in receiving condolences, and their words or their consoling intent may have been more healing than my comparatively silent but supportive presence. But the plague of AIDS cured me of being satisfied with facile comments about God's will or "what's best" or heaven. I still search for words of comfort: God's eternal embrace, death as a kind of healing from suffering, or how the loved one lives on in those she or he touched. The plague of AIDS taught me how lame such words can be in the face of overwhelming grief; it's like falling off a cliff and having someone hand you a flower on the way down.

The most honest thing I can say is, "I'm sorry for your loss." But when I clumsily offered it to a woman who had just lost her husband, not knowing what else to say, one of her sons inadvertently laughed, and I realized I had spouted what has been made cliché by too many crime and forensic shows on TV.

Prolonged suffering and its shadow of death needs a *listening* silence. With other well-meaning clergy on the Spiritual Advisory Committee of AIDS Project Los Angeles, I helped coordinate a retreat on spirituality for those living with HIV and AIDS. After a day of Buddhist mindfulness meditation, Christian *lectio divina*, New Age and New Thought affirmations, and faith-based conversations on illness and dying, we thought we had done pretty well equipping those living with AIDS and their caregivers. But we received a very angry letter from a friend of mine who attended, wanting to know how the hell he was supposed to be spiritual when he's cleaning up his lover's vomit and trying to hold back his own while in absolute terror of what was next. I felt like the Jewish philosopher Martin Buber when a student of his committed suicide just after their visit together. Buber realized he had not been adequately present, and developed his whole I-Thou philosophy of relationship, replacing our usual subject-object ways of relating with subject-subject relationship. We had been so quick to offer the spiritual "tools of the trade" that we failed to begin with a silence that listened for the real questions our own "students" might have asked during that retreat. In reality, they could have been *our* teachers.

People living with HIV and AIDS were our teachers when I participated in a retreat at a Catholic center run by an order of nuns in a rural area outside Detroit. I was amazed at the effort many of the participants put into attending as I helped carry all their medical paraphernalia from their cars to their rooms. I thought of the times when those with fewer challenges simply blew off a retreat because it was "inconvenient." Facing the possibility of death, these AIDS pioneers could teach us all about valuing opportunities to reflect on life and draw on spiritual resources. During a break in the gathering, I walked along a pathway that, unbeknownst to me, led to a cemetery. I found there a mirror of what we were experiencing in our own plague of AIDS. I happened onto a long row of tombstones marking the graves of nuns, young and old, that bore the same year of death: 1918, the year of the worldwide flu pandemic.

I remember a dinner party that included a writer for *The Los Angeles Times* when I wish I had remained silent and listened more. A friend had arranged my participation in hopes that the journalist could help me publish my first book. It was all gay men and the conversation gravitated toward AIDS, and how people with AIDS had been rejected and abandoned by their lovers and friends. Piqued by this defamation of gay men's characters, not realizing this was more than a theoretical or hearsay conversation, I declared the opposite had been my experience—that gay men had generally rallied round their friends. I learned later that the writer I was to meet had AIDS and had indeed been rejected and abandoned by many of his friends! I had failed to realize that those outside the religious community had a very different experience of AIDS and, instead of befriending the writer, I had alienated him. Not long after, he died in the room of an AIDS-care facility next door to a friend I was tending.

It is in the silence, in the listening, that a gesture or word may have a dramatic and consoling effect. As I tended that friend in the room next to the journalist, a squeeze of his hand as I prayed aloud with him was the only indication of consciousness, and I found it comforting. And, in another instance, when another friend was dying, I am told that he began, "Tell Chris Glaser that . . ." but he drifted off before completing a coherent sentence. Nonetheless, to be remembered by someone in his final moments is a gift of unsurpassed value.

Senses of faith (not merely "eyes of faith") or openness to fresh understandings of the spiritual are needed to discern hidden waters in the wilderness of plague. Earlier I described a friend who mourned that "nothing spiritual happened" when his best friend died of AIDS—no rustling of the curtains, no meaningful last words, no spirit ascending to the heavens. My own view of what the spiritual is in such moments is the gathering of friends round the bedside, caring, loving, touching, grieving.

Sometimes the sense of faith is not eyes or ears or feelings; sometimes it is that sixth sense that we tend to deny or rationalize out of the realm of possibility. A friend who is a rabbi awoke in the middle of the night, sensing a masculine presence in her room which was alarming until she realized it was a friendly presence— only to discover the next morning that a close friend had died of AIDS at the very time she had been awakened. Scott Rogo, the parapsychologist of whom I wrote earlier, told me that such a phenomenon is fairly common within populations or communities experiencing widespread death: the boundary between life and death is less solid, more permeable and fluid.

I never counted those I knew who died of AIDS, as did the hospice chaplain I described earlier who kept a count of the 400 clients he had accompanied in their final moments. I was intentional about this, because I did not want to treat them as statistics. Though early in the AIDS crisis I had unsuccessfully argued that my church job description be rewritten with an AIDS focus, anticipating the need, I subsequently found myself "pacing" my involvement, recognizing the dangers of becoming overwhelmed by death and an exclusive focus on AIDS. I dedicated my third book, a book of prayers entitled *Coming Out to God*, to those I knew who had lived with or were living with HIV and AIDS, listing them by first name. I was stunned how many there were, and that was early, in 1991. I have wondered if that's why the book developed a following in the HIV/AIDS community. Many of the prayers were specifically Christian, and so I was thrilled when a rabbi told me he had used the book with his own congregation, admitting with a smile the need to adapt them. I mention this here because one of my discoveries about a "plague" like AIDS was the camaraderie that developed among care-receivers and care-givers alike, regardless of sexuality, religion, class, race, or gender. Though there were exceptions, even medical personnel—doctors, nurses, administrators, candy stripers, custodians—often, by compassionate choice, got caught up in our passionate war on AIDS. Just as in the military a "band of brothers" is melded by war, so we had our own band of brothers and sisters shaped by the common enemy of AIDS. Lesbians, who had their own battles to fight with breast and ovarian cancers, stood in solidarity with us.

I realized how "spoiled" I was in this regard when I was surprised to discover, by contrast, seemingly heartless and sometimes cruel surgeons and oncologists treating my father when he developed lung cancer. And I remember bitter resentment voiced through the media about the AIDS Quilt, asking, "Why don't we have a cancer quilt?" —as if people living and dying with AIDS were getting "special" treatment instead of acknowledging that the majority culture was just not as moved and passionate about cancer as we were about HIV and AIDS. Now we see movements around women's health, and the red ribbons of AIDS are joined by the pink ribbons of cancers that endanger women. Both the women's and the gay communities have learned from their respective plagues that attention and money for research and treatment only come to those who "rage against the dying of the light."

At least I could take "comfort" in the awareness that I was in the same boat with all my friends—that is, until I tested negative for HIV. I was incredibly and even joyously grateful, just as I had been at the time of the first Vietnam era draft lottery upon discovering my number was too high to be called. But immediately I felt survivor's guilt; I felt out of community with all my friends still facing the dangers of HIV infection. Just as in the earlier instance I had felt all the more the need to protest the Vietnam War through writing, education, and demonstrations, so I felt in the second instance more deeply the need to serve where I could in the war with AIDS.

When I mentioned to a close friend with HIV my feeling that my bonds with my brothers had felt broken by testing HIV-negative, he admonished, "But we need you to survive to tell our story." I took this to heart and wrote a novel in 1990 entitled *The Cure: A Post-AIDS Love Story.* Though never published, this futuristic and intentionally hopeful book began with the announcement that a cure had been found for AIDS. Remarkably it presaged the drug "cocktail" of the late 1990s by being a combination of remedies that led to similar social changes, from people returning to work to the reappearance of risky sex, as well as the disheartening news that the cure worked less well for women and racial minorities and that the battlefront had switched to Africa.

Though in no way comparable from a literary standpoint, I frankly had in mind Albert Camus' insightful work *The Plague,* and in homage I quoted from its final pages.

> . . . *Dr. Rieux resolved to compile this chronicle, so that he should not be one of those who hold their peace but should bear witness in favor of those plague-stricken people; so that some memorial of the injustice and outrage done them might endure; and to state quite simply what we learn in time of pestilence: that there are more things to admire in men than to despise. Nonetheless, he knew that the tale he had to tell could not be one of a final victory. It could be only the record of what had had to be done, and what assuredly would have to be done again in the never ending fight against terror and its relentless onslaughts, despite their personal afflictions, by all who, while unable to be saints but refusing to bow down to pestilences, strive their utmost to be healers.*

During a shared devotion, a friend read St. Brigid of Sweden's description of Christ on the cross, and, in sudden recognition, I burst out, "Sounds like she's describing a person in the final stages of AIDS." My friend pointed out that she had lived during the time of the Plague, and could have as easily been describing one of its victims.

There was also a parallel to the experience of the elderly attending one funeral service after another, with the exception that people who died of AIDS had more surviving friends and family to mourn their loss. My biggest fear anticipating my own death had always been that I would have to say goodbye to all my friends. The plague of AIDS thrust me into that experience prematurely, but instead of *me* leaving, it was them. A prayer I wrote at the time compared losing friends with AIDS to sand slipping through my fingers over which I had no control. After awhile, a kind of numbness took over, and many of us found ourselves grieving that we could not adequately mourn each friend who died of AIDS. My friends and I shared a gallows humor, telling each other at funerals, "We've got to stop meeting like this." Maybe it was a combination of whistling in the dark and seeking joy to balance our grief that those funerals often were true celebrations of the departed's life: part wake with funny stories, part stage production with pop-music recordings, self-made videos, releasing of balloons, and distributing of flowers.

Though the solid nature of grey tombstones gives me comfort as I enjoy occasional strolls through cemeteries, the AIDS Quilt became a colorful alternative. I have seen various partial displays of the Quilt, but the most incredible was seeing it in its entirety in front of the Washington Monument in D.C. I was honored to bring a panel of the partner of a friend. And I discovered still other friends as I walked among the rows of carefully and caringly prepared cloth panels that represented the lives taken by AIDS. One that stood out, one I subsequently wrote about, was that of Chris Chlanda. He was represented by his own panel, as well as a couple of other quilt panels representing groups of friends and employees of a particular San Francisco bar. We had been close friends at Yale, and he had helped arrange a dinner to introduce me to the medieval historian and Yale professor John Boswell. I was serving on a Presbyterian task force on homosexuality and ordination, and Boswell was just completing a manuscript that would subsequently be published under the title, *Christianity, Social Tolerance and Homosexuality*. I was so impressed with what Boswell was discovering in his research that I arranged a meeting between him and the task force. They, too, were astonished at his findings, which in turn positively influenced our report. Boswell and I became friends and, when I left New Haven to serve in ministry in southern California, he came to Los Angeles at my request to give lectures on several occasions. As I stood in front of Chris Chlanda's quilt panel, I understood how one hospitable act of his had reverberations of grace far beyond what might have been imagined. And I couldn't help but think that his life and each of our lives are filled with many such moments in which, by being kind, by being hospitable, we reach far beyond our finite capacities to change the world.

If only I always kept that thought before me! My last encounter with John Boswell was not a positive one. I had just endured some rough times emotionally and I was just re-learning to stand up for myself. I had left early from a rare and significant reunion of old friends to drive a great distance to take Boswell to dinner for his birthday while he was on a speaking trip to Los Angeles. I was really looking forward to being together again and taking him to dinner at one of West Hollywood's trendier restaurants. This was in the days before cell phones were in common use, so I called him from the lobby of his hotel when I arrived, little knowing he was waiting for me outside another entrance. I had arrived a few minutes late because I had gone to the wrong hotel, and the additional time I wasted in going to a different location made me anxious, but made John angry—so angry that he delivered sharp words that deeply hurt when we managed to locate one another. As I said, I was just recovering from hurtful treatment, and I wasn't about to put up with it. I asked, "Are you going to be angry all night? Because if you are, I'd rather not be with you." He said, "Fine!" and stormed away. I never saw him again. I felt proud that I stood up for myself, at the same time devastated that the birthday plans I had for him were ruined. On the phone with a friend later that night, we pondered if he had developed a "star mentality" since our last encounter.

When I once was critical of closeted pastors who didn't support the gay movement, Boswell had sympathetically replied, "Who knows what bears are in their caves?" I didn't know what bears were in Boswell's cave. I didn't know he had AIDS and would die before I saw him again. A mutual friend tried to effect a reconciliation, to which John replied, "I only have positive thoughts." This proved no comfort, as I wondered what he meant: did he only have positive thoughts of me or did he not want to think of me at all?

I wish now that every time someone gets angry with me I could ask, "Who knows what bears are in their cave?" and move on. I will never forgive myself that I let John spend possibly his last birthday alone. If only I had gone on with the evening, things would have calmed down and we would have had a good time. What a fool I was.

One Easter, at a time when the AIDS crisis felt so overwhelming to me that I was desperate for hope, the worship service and pastor's sermon of my church did not satisfy. I went for a walk that afternoon along the shore, a sanctuary whose aisle of sand I have always walked with greater anticipation than aisles of more traditional sanctuaries. The sky was bright blue, the winds crisp, and the waves translucent. The beauty made me glad to be alive, but did not answer the questions of my heart. At the conclusion of the walk I entered a pub for some warming coffee, and happened onto a friend I had not seen in years. I was happy to be updated on his spiritual quest and to learn that he was in a relationship. But when I asked about the partner, my friend said simply, "He died last week." Once again, I had cause for despair. But he continued, "He was diagnosed two years ago, and he used what time he had left to help others. It was wonderful to see. We had a good time together. I have no regrets. He died in my arms. I felt him leave his body. That's why I'm sure I'll see him again." When we parted, I thanked him for delivering the Easter message I needed to hear.

Another lifeline came from my friend Pat Hoffman long before she became a chaplain for an AIDS agency and wrote a book about her experience entitled *AIDS and the Sleeping Church*. She introduced me to Etty Hillesum's wartime diary *An Interrupted Life*, telling me she thought it might be helpful in coping with the pandemic. Once again, another historical experience of plague spoke to my own experience. This time the plague was Nazism; the virus, anti-Semitism. Etty Hillesum kept a journal as she came of age sexually, journalistically, and aesthetically just before Nazi Germany overshadowed her Danish homeland. As I read the first one-hundred pages, I found it interesting, but wondered why Pat thought it would be helpful in the AIDS crisis. But then Etty began to mature spiritually as she faced the Nazi danger, including "relocation" to one of Germany's concentration camps. When Jews in Denmark were forced to wear yellow Stars of David, she praised a fellow Jew for going "the extra mile" in his self-affirmation: "That man in the Beethovenstraat this afternoon won't get a mention in [history books]. I looked at him as one might at the first crocus in spring, with pure enchantment. He was wearing a huge golden star, wearing it triumphantly on his chest. He was a procession and a demonstration all by himself as he cycled along so happily. And all that yellow—I suddenly had a poetic vision of the sun rising above him, so radiant and smiling did he look." This particular story makes me think of t-shirts that proudly bore the words, "HIV POSITIVE."

"I am with the hungry, with the ill-treated and the dying, every day, but I am also with the jasmine and with that piece of sky beyond my window; there is room for everything in a single life. For belief in God and for a miserable end," Etty claims a sense of equilibrium in the face of virulent madness. And, as she anticipated being transported into Germany, she boldly prays, "Dear God, these are anxious times. Tonight for the first time I lay in the dark with burning eyes as scene after scene of human suffering passed before me. I shall promise You one thing, God, just one very small thing: I shall never burden my today with cares about my tomorrow, although that takes some practice. Each day is sufficient unto itself. I shall try to help you, God, to stop my strength ebbing away, though I cannot vouch for it in advance. But one thing is becoming increasingly clear to me: that you cannot help us, that we must help You to help ourselves. And that is all we can manage these days and also all that really matters: that we safeguard that little piece of You, God, in ourselves. And perhaps in others as well."

I want to quote much of the book to you, the reader—that's how profoundly Etty's words spoke to my heart. I recognized her experience of helplessness as my own. I could do nothing to save my friends from a miserable death, even as I might make it a little less miserable by refusing to abandon them. Over and over again, Etty's words brought tears to my eyes. But what made me cry was not my own helplessness, but the helplessness of God. Death by plague—whether war, disease, bigotry, or old age—made clear "that we must help [God] to help ourselves . . . that we safeguard that little piece of . . . God in ourselves. And perhaps in others as well." Her words echo Teresa of Avila, who said that on earth "God's body must be our own." As a congregation in San Francisco with which I worked affirmed, "God has no hands but our hands, God has no feet but our feet, God has no face but our own."

In her most terrible anguish, Etty could yet affirm, "There will always be a small patch of sky above, and there will always be enough space to fold two hands in prayer." More than personal presence and practical help, prayer was the most vital thing I had to offer those who were suffering.

AIDS is still devastating communities throughout the developing nations, especially Africa. And minority populations and younger generations in the developed world are learning anew what we learned during the most intense, scariest, plague-like years of the AIDS crisis that I directly experienced. Even today it surprises me to hear, through networking sites like Facebook, that those I knew then are still alive, as I have presumed so many of my friends, colleagues, and acquaintances of the time were dead. Even those infected in those days are living decades thanks to the new AIDS drugs. I am astonished to meet people who have never lost anyone to AIDS. What I have written here are the echoes of the pandemic for me, a pandemic that still reverberates around the globe. AIDS taught me firsthand compassion for all those throughout history and throughout the world who have suffered or are suffering similar enormous losses of life. It taught me impatience with institutions and individuals that refuse to acknowledge what's happening. But it also taught me community: the importance of pulling together to address a crisis with everything we've got, including our spirituality.

One final story: my friend and colleague in ministry, Steve Pieters, was diagnosed with AIDS a few years after we met in 1982. Given an experimental treatment that killed everyone else in one of the earliest clinical trials, he survives to this day, having beaten back lymphoma, Kaposi's sarcoma, and other opportunistic infections. Before I tested negative for HIV, in the midst of my own terrors of the disease and of death, I had a significant dream. I wrote earlier that one of my favorite films is Frank Capra's *Lost Horizon*, which depicts a narrow entryway from the storm-ravaged Himalayas into a peaceful and verdant valley of spiritual equanimity and social well-being. In the dream, Steve led me into a vividly blue pool of water in the shadow of great mountains. The pool had the shape and size of a grave. There were steps down into it, like a church baptismal for full immersion. As he led me down into the cool, refreshing water, the horizontal opening became a vertical doorway. The blue of the water became the deep blue of the sky, and, as the stairs continued to descend, I saw a beautiful green valley awaiting us below. This dream seemed so real! It gave me such peace and joy! I awoke in tears of gratitude.

Chapter Seven
Precipitous Death

Much death seems precipitous—too quick, too soon, too young, too "arbitrary." Much as in the case of inadvertent death that I wrote of earlier, my personal concern would be what role I might play in an accidental or "premature" death, mine or someone else's. "There are no accidents," is a popular thing to believe these days, but, while I do have more and more experiences of synchronicity as I grow older—when coincidences seem to run deeper than mere chance, or things seem to line up supernaturally well—I believe that such an attitude does not adequately take spontaneity or the random nature of the universe into account. It reminds me too much of someone in my fundamentalist upbringing declaring, "This must be God's will."

As I put the final touches on this manuscript, the local media reported that a four-year-old boy was slain by a stray bullet fired in celebration of the new year of 2010 while he sat in a pew during a church watch service. In its fall back to earth, the bullet penetrated the sanctuary roof and then the boy. How does one make sense of this?

I cannot make sense of most precipitous deaths, in and of themselves, other than to mark the fragility of life. In college I sat with a friend's family and her boyfriend as she underwent surgery to remove and diagnose a tumor in her breast, not knowing if the breast would be there when she woke up. The tumor was benign, the relief was great, but she was subsequently killed in a car accident. Each of three friends of mine took enormous fatherly pride in their daughters, one sending Christmas cards each year of him with his daughter in yet another exotic vacation spot. In one case, the father died abruptly and in the other two cases the daughters died young, one in a car accident and the other at the hands of a former boyfriend. Often the only thing precipitous death teaches us is my mother's parting advice whenever we left the house, "Be careful!," which my brother always found funny, as if we wouldn't be careful without her parting words.

Then there are wars filled with courageous, patriotic, but also precipitous occasions for death—World War II in my parents' generation, Korea in another, Vietnam in mine, Iraq and Afghanistan in the present. Why was my father saved from combat in Japan because of the atomic bomb? Why did my Aunt Jackie lose her first husband in Korea? Why was my number in the first Vietnam draft lottery too high to be drafted? Why is my nephew's military expertise more valuable in Washington than in Iraq? It's the proverbial saying of the end times, "One shall be taken, and the other left." These days, as I watch the final moments of the PBS news and grieve each name and photograph of those who die in our present wars, I can't make sense of why these particular individuals had to die, while I honor their sacrifice to serve in harm's way.

And then there are those who die as the result of both natural and unnatural disasters. Katrina was a natural disaster; the Holocaust, or Shoah, was an unnatural disaster. Such deaths were not only precipitous but preventable and, as with war, culturally we play them over and over again in our minds to make sense of them through documentaries, dramas, books, and films. Instead of wringing our hands, we wring our consciences—what did we do? What could we have done? How did we fail? And the "we" here is the entire human race. In the face of such unexplainable tragedies, our culture parallels the obsessive-compulsive, replaying the suffering over and over again almost as if hoping for a different outcome. Or maybe it's simply grief's need to return because we can't accept it all at once.

Whatever meaning is to be had of a particular death is determined, I believe, by context. "He was a hero." "She was faithful." "It was tragic." "It was a sacrifice of love." Even in precipitous death we try to find such meaning, but it's harder. In my personal life, what such death has taught me has sometimes been indirect, introducing a kind of Rube Goldberg effect in my life, where one thing led to another and to another, and so on.

One fatal accident that taught me something about myself, however indirectly, happened to someone I had only met once. But just as anything we do in our lives, no matter how small, may have a ripple effect in strangers' lives, so this death played a role in my own coming of age. Just before a rare daytime football game, I happened to see a friend from high school choir who told me his family was worried about his older brother, who had driven up to their mountain cabin the night before, but had not phoned upon arrival as usual. The following Monday I learned that Chris's brother had gone over a cliff and was dead. His death prompted me to reach out to Chris.

I had always wanted to be his friend, but thought he was way too cool for me. Yet his brother's death overcame my fears of unworthiness and of rejection. We became friends, and he introduced me to Roman Catholicism and I introduced him to Youth for Christ, where he eventually was moved "to accept Jesus Christ as his personal savior." He had told me how confusing his experience in Roman Catholic schools was. In elementary school the nuns taught him the biblical stories; but in junior high, the priests taught him they were not true. The fundamentalism of Youth for Christ was just the tonic he needed to rejuvenate his childhood faith. He became part of a small weekly Bible study of like-minded friends, using the paraphrased versions of the scriptures that were later assembled as *The Living Bible.* When Chris did not prove a regular at these meetings, I felt a certain emptiness. I wanted to grow close to Chris even as I wanted to grow close to Christ. My sexual and spiritual impulses were intertwined, which could feel wonderful and awful at the same time. Adolescent hormones were raging, troubled waters that Gore Vidal once characterized in a youth of sixteen in the opening scene of the historical novel, *Washington, D.C.* Blissfully out in a rainstorm, dodging streaks of lightning, the youth is aware of his contradictory urges to fight or make love—both erotic in their desire for intimate engagement.

Only later would I discover words to describe my "urge to merge," with Chris or with Christ. Eros, I would learn, fuels all desire for intimacy, whether with God or another person. And desire for intimacy may inspire or shame, because intimacy requires stripping naked before the subject of one's desire, incredibly freeing but also incredibly vulnerable and potentially embarrassing. (I intentionally have chosen "subject of one's desire" rather than "object of one's desire" because I believe that in true intimacy the initiator must offer him/herself vulnerably as object.) Intimacy itself requires a death of sorts—thus in the Christian myth people are drawn close to God through the death of Christ and drawn close to Christ through the death of self, and in the Dionysian myth he and his lovers are drawn together by the death of Dionysus. But death gives way to life and love. Christ is crucified and Dionysus is torn apart, and yet both are resurrected. These are mythological responses to otherwise unexplainable precipitous death, the first revealing the nature of compassion and the second revealing the nature of passion.

Both prayer making and lovemaking involve a loss of self, of separate identity—that is, I believe, if done right! To forget for a moment that I am a discrete being—or better, to remember for a moment that I am one with all—is the goal of both mystic and lover, of spiritual ecstasy and sexual orgasm. Charismatic sects laud being "slain in the spirit" and being given over to speaking in tongues—losing control as in a sexual climax. Even one as counter-orthodox in his Christian views as Bishop John Spong has recently written of death as the realization of our unity with all things holy in his book, *Eternal Life: A New Vision: Beyond Religion, Beyond Theism, Beyond Heaven and Hell.*

Chris's brother's death had brought us together as friends, but different colleges separated us until an echo of his brother's death sounded in Chris's own serious traffic accident. His brush with death brought me back to his side, and we became friends again despite our separate paths. One Christmas night he confounded me by confessing he smoked pot. What disappointed me was that we had not shared the experience and so, though I had never taken any interest in drugs, I immediately wanted to try it. We drove around North Hollywood smoking joints. Later, we tried hallucinogens together. The euphoria of those experiences would never match the euphoria I would experience when I finally let myself have sex, first with a woman, and eventually with men. Though never physically intimate, the drugs were ways to let go of self and be close to Chris. A few years ago, my brother sent me an obituary for someone with Chris's name, a sobering clipping. The age was right and he was buried in the same cemetery as his brother, but the biography didn't match, and I chose to believe it wasn't Chris. The friendship died long ago, but what I learned from the precipitous nature of his brother's death was that I could love a man in a way that most men could love a woman, and that such love was also a gift of God. His brother's seemingly meaningless death perhaps had as many meanings as there were contexts to understand it, including mine.

In college a friend with whom I had been close in junior high but had not seen recently was injured in the first practice scrimmages of his Christian college football team. Karl Conley was like many I chose to befriend: not popular, taunted for his lazy eye, a struggling student, and from a class unacceptable to our peers. He lived in the garage of his family home, it being so small, though he was an only child. One time when I visited him, his father sat in the living room in nothing but his briefs, and then came out to chat with my parents when they picked me up. My mother's only comment was that he might have put on a pair of pants when he came outside. Karl was good-hearted, had a unique fondness for Civil War battle history, and could kick a football farther than anyone on our team. I have a film of one of his kicks, almost the length of the field. I was pleased to hear he had gotten into college as well as making the school's football team. But in summer practice, he got hit pretty hard, and though he got up, he keeled over suddenly and was rushed to a hospital. Apparently he had an aneurism that, according to the doctor, would not have needed much to set it off—merely scratching his head might have caused disaster. But Karl was still alive, though unconscious, and I remember praying hard for him that he would recover.

A premature report of his death caused a visceral response in me. After being told mistakenly that he had died, I went in the bathroom and looked at myself in the mirror, seeing my reflection almost as an impressionist painting, so unreal everything seemed. Why him and not me? I wondered. When later I realized reports of his death had been wrong, I laughed out loud, thinking, "I can't wait to tell Karl what happened! What a laugh we'll have." But it wasn't to be. Karl died, this time for real. There is no point to this story, and perhaps that's the nature of precipitous death. Except to say, it made me aware that I was lucky to be alive. And to say, I wish we had not lost touch as we went off to different schools. One of my excuses for not maintaining contact was an unfortunate remark he had made about a teacher's sexuality that made me think he would be unaccepting of me, and I thought at the time, "How dare he, when I have befriended him when others wouldn't?" How indecorous of me.

John Rice was a United Methodist minister that I met at a conference I had organized. This is a story of failing to pay attention, of failing to be mindful, of failing literally to listen. Out of gratitude he wrote a song for me and sent me the tape, to which I never got around to listening. We dated briefly but there were no sparks for me. We became friends and remained so for more than a decade. Attending the funeral of a friend, my partner pointed to a hymn in the bulletin written by John and whose tune was named for me! "Did you know about this?" he asked. I had not known. It was the song John had sent me, entitled, "Walk With Me." I was honored as I sang the song for the first time. I realized how inattentive I had been.

By that time, John had met Brian Davidson, a member of West Hollywood Presbyterian Church, and they had moved to Knoxville, Tennessee. After I moved with my partner to Atlanta, John and Brian came for our marriage ceremony in our neighborhood Presbyterian Church. They stayed with us and together enjoyed an impromptu "bachelors' party" at a local bar the night before the ceremony. They spoke about how much they too would like to have a public ceremony celebrating their union. Two weeks later, John was dead. He had had a fender-bender with a fellow church member, and as they exchanged insurance information, a young man in a truck raced down the frontage road and pinned John against his own car, which the momentum of the truck continued to climb, crushing him to death. Brian was advised against seeing the body afterward. We were all devastated, especially of course, Brian.

A few weeks after, I spoke at Columbia Theological Seminary in Decatur, adjacent to Atlanta, to a packed dining area, about the need for acceptance of gay people in the church. One woman asked a question. She prefaced it by saying there was a gay couple, active leaders in her home church, that was not out. One of the couple had died in an accident, and her fellow church members did not understand the depth of the survivor's grief, thinking they were "just" roommates. I was stunned. "Where is your home church?" I asked the woman. "Knoxville," she replied. She was from John and Brian's church. I used John's precipitous death as a teachable moment, believing it was more than coincidence that his and Brian's tragedy would surface in a question and answer period with students preparing to become pastors in denominations that, as I had in my inattention to John's gift of a song, fail to appreciate the gifts of their gay members.

Three times in my life I have had an inkling of what those who suffer precipitous deaths might experience—three times when I felt on the brink of personal disaster: once in junior high, once on the way to seminary, and once while I was writing this book. Hiking in the hills surrounding my junior high school with a friend, I slipped on loose shale and tumbled head over heels down to the bottom of a narrow ravine cut out of the slope by erosion. Sharp rocks on each side slashed my body while dried underbrush scratched my skin. Something inside me told me to relax and follow the pull of gravity—possibly why I incurred no broken bones trying to resist. Down at the bottom, I inspected myself. Shock prevented me from immediately feeling pain, but I could see the seriousness of my wounds, at the same time awed that I had not been knocked out by the plunge. When my friend caught up with me, he said, "I thought you were a goner!"

Driving across country from the West Coast to the East Coast to attend seminary, I had a similar experience along I-40 in New Mexico. On a night when a driving rain limited visibility, I came up on a car too fast and stepped on my brakes. They must've been wet, because they caught too quickly and sent me into a tailspin with cars and semis coming toward me at full speed. My parents, following me as far as Kansas to visit relatives, looked on with horror as I spun on the highway in front of oncoming traffic. I remembered to drive in the direction of the skid, but with few points of reference and blinding rain I wasn't sure which way that was. The steering wheel seemed to have its own mind and I let go of it, wondering how all this would turn out. I ended up in the median strip with only my starter engine damaged. Kind strangers stopped to help, including the driver of a formidable semi with two trailers that could have as easily plowed into my VW.

I wrote of these two incidents in an earlier book, describing the peace I felt despite the precipitous danger surrounding me.

I wrote that "Deep within us, I believe, runs a wellspring of intuitive trust and faith in the cosmos and Creator." I wrote about my need to let go of control and trust God, vocationally and personally. I still believe this, but a third incident added another dimension to that trust. Writing this book has been a challenge, to put it mildly. Death is not an easy subject, especially when removed from the abstract and made personal, as I have done in these chapters. My other work plus my exercise schedule has had a therapeutic effect. So, while working on the previous chapter, I went for my usual long run. Along my route there is one intersection with no traffic signal where Atlanta drivers (notorious for killing pedestrians) do not stop for people in the crosswalk. Thus I'm always cautious crossing. A delivery truck surprised me by stopping for me as I approached. I had seen no cars behind the truck, so my chief concern now was the traffic flowing from the opposite direction. Immediately a gap was available and I ran for it, when suddenly I realized a car was whizzing past the delivery truck at top speed. Both driver and I were on a collision course, and I realized that I was about to be hit hard, disabled for life if not killed outright. I pulled myself back, thinking that his side rearview mirror, passing me at full speed, might still rip me open. I pulled up just fast enough that I missed the passing car by less than an inch, even as his tires and that of the car behind him screeched on the asphalt. The only person to yell was the driver behind the principal car, and he was yelling at the precipitous stop of the driver ahead. All I could think to say was, "This is an intersection." I was absolutely calm. And once I realized that neither car had hit, I continued my run.

I had recently read Malcolm Gladwell's *Blink: The Power of Thinking without Thinking*, and I realized the research he reported on had been true in this case. In dire emergencies, time seems to slow down, attention is extremely focused, judgments are split-second, and, when bodily harm is threatened, the only thing that matters is extricating oneself quickly. Rolling down the hill in junior high and spinning on an interstate in New Mexico, I had experienced things in slow motion, feeling *very* present, and seemingly without thinking, letting go—the better strategy in those circumstances. In the running incident, seconds seemed to stretch into a long time; I was extremely focused, but, seemingly without thinking, pulled back, avoiding injury. If I had "let go" in that case, I would have been hurt. I still had control.

All this is to imagine what it must be like for those facing a precipitous death. However unexpected, the moment may feel stretched—Einstein's theory of relativity holds here physiologically. Mindfulness is not an optional form of meditation in such a circumstance; it is required. And what to do in response is determined in Gladwell's "blink of an eye," whether that is to relax or resist.

I find this strangely comforting. Save for those who absolutely don't know what hit them, others who faced a precipitous death were not kept completely powerless. They may have had both time and awareness to experience it and, while their whole lives may not have flashed before them, they held the conscious knowledge that writer Kazantzakis' friend Zorba the Greek wanted at the end of his life: "that right until the very last minute I was in full possession of my senses." And, just as Zorba thought of his friend in that moment, likely they thought of those they loved. There have been many such stories that confirm the latter: the pinned down victim of a train accident drawing a heart with his own blood, the lengthy note written to his family by a passenger as his plane went down, the final calls from those under attack in planes and buildings on 9/11.

And—and I know all of this is speculative—they also had a choice how to respond: to relax or resist. Many of those on board United Flight 93 over Pennsylvania apparently resisted the terrorists. Reports are that many on the sinking Titanic chose to sing a hymn. Failed resistance is still a victory of sorts. And acceptance is not a defeat. To the end, they refused to let circumstances define them. Like Sartre's victim looking his tormentors in the eye, they claimed their dignity and thus, their lives, even in death.

Chapter Eight
Death Made Personal

Death of My Parents

During my father's retirement dinner, my mother saw the server carrying drinks to others in the large private dining room of the restaurant. My parents were tee totaling Baptists, but my mother thought the margaritas looked refreshing. She surprised me by asking, "If I order one of those and don't like it, will you finish it for me?" My sister and I, being the only drinkers of our immediate family, had chosen not to order wine out of respect for my parents' religious principles. When my mother turned to my father to check it out with him, I was certain that that would be the end of it. To my astonishment, they both ordered margaritas and so my sister and I felt free to have wine, though I ended up finishing off my mother's drink as well. Dad finished his drink as one of his co-workers, in the formal part of the reception, chided him, "Now, you ask Wayne for the time, and he'll build you a watch." The man captured Dad's love of storytelling (even to those who may have already heard the stories!), while the margaritas signified Mom's adventurous spirit, a willingness to try something even if it bent the rules.

That spunk may have lost Mom a job as a first-grade teacher at a rigid fundamentalist school after thirty years of underpaid but dedicated teaching. (Our family also wondered if my coming out had anything to do with her not being invited back to teach the following year.) Though beloved by her students and fellow teachers, her principal, who had just been given sole authority to let teachers go, was an unhappy woman who seemed to resent anyone having either fun or independence. When I won an award in college, the school paper asked for a story about it for their alumni section. My mother provided the brief piece, along with a photograph of me, then sporting a beard. The school would not publish a picture of me with a beard and my mother, who didn't like the beard either, nonetheless took the story back, saying, "He won the award with the beard, and if you don't want the picture, you don't get the story."

I inherited my father's storytelling gene and my mother's adventurous spirit. Not surprisingly, when it came to religion, my father loved to teach the Bible's stories and my mom loved to read the mystics—of any religion. Now those who know me know where I got these predilections. My parents were high school sweethearts from a small college town in Kansas who both worked on the school paper. Dad was the editor and Mom was the treasurer. Events separated them three times, and I have their correspondence carried on when Dad went to Iowa for work in the 1930's at a meat packing plant and later travelled to California, working as a truck driver for a bread company. He proposed to her from a public phone in a small hotel in Quincy, a town in the Sierra Nevada mountain range. In 1939, they were married in the First Baptist Church of Pittsburg, Kansas, visiting her family in the town and then his family across the border on their 80-acre farm in Missouri, before moving to northern California. On the drive across country, my mother saw her first mountains. After my sister, Sharon, was born, Dad was drafted, and eventually became part of the occupying forces in Japan, and this third separation provided the final batch of letters between them. They were now living in southern California, and my brother Steve would be born in my father's absence. In one of my favorite letters, Mom describes being able to see the "H" in the Hollywood sign from her hospital room. Now, as I read Dad's very long letters of tiny script, I have to remind myself he was only eighteen when he wrote the ones from Iowa and twenty-nine when writing from Japan. He had a gift as a writer.

For their 50th wedding anniversary, my sister, brother, and I coordinated a reception for them after worship at the First Baptist Church of North Hollywood. Their church held most of their friends, and it was a chance for the whole family to be in church together once more as well. The preacher talked about them in the sermon, and we had sent invitations featuring their wedding photo from 1939 to other friends from work, school, and the community. After the reception, the extended family gathered in a private room of a nearby steak house for midday dinner. We jointly gave them a trip on Amtrak's Coast Starlight that runs along the West Coast from Los Angeles to Vancouver, with an excursion to Victoria Island. After all those cross-country road trips along Route 66 to visit relatives in the Midwest, this would be the last trip they would take together. And for once, Dad didn't have to drive.

Eighteen months after our celebration Dad died from lung cancer. He had survived another type of malignant cancer when I was in college, but he had been a smoker most of his life and it took its toll. For months after his death, I wanted to rip cigarettes out of people's mouths; I was so angry about their death-dealing effect on people. What was also upsetting was how my father was treated by his doctors. I mentioned in chapter 6, "Death by Plague," how compassionate I found the doctors engaged in treating the AIDS pandemic. My father's doctors were the opposite, cold and dispassionate. On one visit to his surgeon's office, the doctor would not even come into the room with us, but stood in the doorway, doing a "good ol' boy" hail-fellow-well-met routine and saying nothing of substance. It felt as if he were afraid to come in; as if dying were "catchy." I believe this was the doctor who once responded to my father's concerns about his death, "Well, we've all got to die sometime."

Now I know a part of my reaction is the old "kill the messenger" response of ancient times, when a messenger bearing bad news was literally slain. I've been with enough people receiving bad medical news to know how picked apart the doctor's words, attitudes, or demeanor can be. But by that time I had had much experience of AIDS doctors, nurses, therapists, and volunteer caregivers who really cared and could show that care through their willingness to touch their patients, sit on their hospital beds, listen to their concerns, give them as much information as possible about their condition and the treatment options, and even give them and their loved ones hugs. My dad may not have wanted so much attention, but a little of this treatment would have been nice. I kept wanting to say to his doctors about their visits, "Once more, with feeling!"

We had hoped to bring my father home to die. We met with hospice staffers to discuss what was required. He had been conscious for breakfast, chatting with my mom. But he was unconscious when I sat with him in the afternoon, giving him water on a sponge, carefully shaving his face with an electric razor as Mom requested, brushing his still black hair that had grown back after chemo. I read Psalms and other scriptures to him in case he could hear. I spoke to him, too, though I don't remember what I said. The most significant conversation we had had during his illness came just after test results showed the cancer had moved into the liver, which meant it was fatal. Mom called to tell me, saying he had taken it hard, and I went over to their house to be with them. Mom left us alone, and we talked about it. We also talked about faith, and his strong fundamentalist faith seemed more yielding and thus all the more real by his frank admissions of doubt about what lay beyond death. This was an "aha" for me, one that deepened my admiration of him. He had always seemed a little afraid of such intimacy, but now his vulnerability could not be hidden.

That night my mother phoned from the hospital, wanting me to come and spend the night with her and Dad. I had just returned from a trip, and had some kind of dysentery that made me very fatigued. But my main reason for asking her to call my sister instead was that I wanted to be there when Dad died, and I thought that was days away. I would not know until we received the hospital bill that the doctor ordered a large dose of morphine that night to speed his death. Now, I have few reservations about such assistance; I had even pressed the partner of a friend with AIDS to accept a morphine drip for his friend as a humane choice. As had been explained to me, the body fights with all its might to stay alive, trying to grasp breath while the lungs fill with fluid. The morphine simply relaxes the body so that it accepts the inevitable. So, the process was not in question for me; it was rather that the doctor did not tell us what he had instructed the nurses to do.

I had taken to sleeping with the phone next to my bed, just in case, but that night I had failed to move it from the living room. The noise of the window air conditioning unit and my sound sleep prevented me from hearing my sister's first phone call and the message she left on the answering machine. An hour later, her second phone call woke me. By the time I arrived at the hospital, Dad's eyes were open and unseeing, but he still breathed and his heart still beat. "Dad, we're here!" I said loudly, believing hearing might still be possible. As always, my mom was still caring for him, hovering around his prone body, stroking his arm and brow, speaking his name occasionally, as I recall, gently pleading for him not to leave her alone. There was a sense of unreality to it, probably a psychic defense mechanism, almost the opposite of a feeling of déjà vu, as if this were something that had not yet happened but was to come.

The 1972 Sylmar quake in California, which rocked our house as our family stood in the doorways of our central hall, was followed by hundreds of aftershocks. But some Californians felt aftershocks when none occurred, including me, and local psychiatrists theorized we had suppressed the terror of the main event when it happened and now were reliving the moment until the terror dissipated. In my experience, that's how grief works as well. The reality, the moment, of death is so traumatic that waves of grief sweep over us for days, weeks, months, and years to come. My father's breathing and heart slowed and stopped, and he was no more. It was like standing in the eye of a hurricane. We had passed through one side of the storm—the spots on his lung x-ray, the biopsy, the diagnosis, the invasive surgery, the chemo visits, the hospitalizations, the spread of the cancer, the fatal prognosis, and, throughout, his suffering to the point that even a hug hurt him and our suffering to the point that even his grace over our last family meal thanking God for "my wonderful family" brought tears to our eyes and pain to our hearts. Now we would pass through the other side of the storm—the loss, the grief, the anger, the self-doubt, the emptiness, and for my mom, the loneliness to follow. But in this moment, there was peace, and a silence like no other.

As the minister in the family it would have been appropriate for me to lead us in a prayer, but I have no recollection of what I did in those moments before and after dad breathed his last. I would have done so with any other family, but just as "a prophet is not without honor except in his own country," so it sometimes is with ministers and their families of origin. Perhaps they know too much about us to think of us as worthy men and women—not so much our sins, which are many, so much as familiarity. Perhaps the same incest taboo intended to inhibit sexual intimacy among family members registers to inhibit spiritual intimacy as well. I had enjoyed a degree of spiritual intimacy with my parents, and if it were just them in the room, I would not have hesitated. But when it came to my siblings, I had reservations. As I say, I don't remember if I led us in a prayer, but prayers were getting said anyway, silently, in all of our hearts. Prayers for Dad, for Mom, for all of us. Maybe Dad for us.

My mom made her final goodbyes. We left the hospital. Later Mom would wonder aloud how she could possibly have left him there that night, even though dead, but we were all dazed by shock and gloom, and the only thing to do was go to our respective homes. I believe my brother Steve took her to his place that night. Dad had died in the early morning hours of July the Fourth, so, the next day, as people all around us readied themselves for whatever Independence Day festivities were at hand, we spent the day looking at caskets, arranging his burial at the cemetery, and meeting with the pastor about the service. Paradoxically, this work seemed pleasurable to me, even fun. I realized more personally than ever how important a ritual making funeral arrangements can be. We mourned, yet there were times of laughter. Touring the casket showroom, we joked that we should each pick out our own caskets now to save future trouble. After selecting a vault at the cemetery, we went to lunch, and the familiarity of having sandwiches at a coffee shop as a family was comforting. Too, we could be ourselves, as spouses and progeny were not with us. It was just the family we had all begun with, with all of our qualities and quirks. When we met with the pastor in the afternoon, my mom asked that "Going Home" be played, because that had become a favorite for them in their final year together. I was given the task of selecting some scriptures that I would read that reflected the unique qualities of Dad's faith. I was grateful to have something to do to honor my father.

I was surprised and touched by the number of my own friends who attended his service at the First Baptist Church. I was moved that a Jewish friend had a tree planted in Israel in his honor, and that a Catholic friend arranged masses to be said in his memory. When I finished reading the scriptures, I placed them in his casket, along with a copy of the book I dedicated to my parents entitled, *Come Home!* His last words to me had been, "When are you coming home?" as I was away when he was hospitalized for the final time, and that phone call was the last I encountered him conscious. He was buried with a scrimshaw tie clip my partner and I had brought him from Martha's Vineyard a few years before and a sporty woolen cap we had brought from Ireland when he initially lost his hair to chemo. I cried on the drive to the cemetery, a sob coming from some unknown depth. It was grief not only at my loss, but his loss as well, never becoming the doctor he had wanted to be due to economic circumstances as well as cultural limitations that said a farm boy from rural Missouri didn't stand a chance, even as a haberdasher from Missouri could become president. One of Dad's proudest possessions was a letter from then Senator Harry Truman that followed his meeting him, an occasion my father used to ask his help getting into West Point. That had not been possible, either.

Beside my father's casket, my mother had poignantly remarked to another church member, "I know it was only his earthly body, but I loved it so!" My mother lived on in the house they shared because she felt her husband's presence there, one manifestation of which was a hummingbird outside the windows of their family room that she had never before seen and associated it with my father's spirit. I wrote in the chapter on AIDS about how mementoes may serve as sacramentals, conveying the presence of those who have passed through our lives. Sometimes enough tangible spiritual links aggregate for one individual so as to create a shrine. Like so many who lose a family member, my mother, at first unconsciously and then quite consciously, created an altar to my father's memory in the year that followed his death. It began with an altar-like wooden portable pump organ that he took to jails to play hymns as part of the jail ministry team from our church. Then his brown leather Bible with its gilt-edge pages; a photo of him and his dog, who died two weeks after he did in his usual position waiting for Dad to come home, lying on the ground, nose pressed in the space between the asphalt of the driveway and the front gate; the ceramic tile of a butterfly that I brought from New Mexico; an anniversary card obviously intended for my mother but found, lost and unsigned, between his desk and the wall after his passing; a vase with a silk flower; a plaque depicting an open Bible with Jesus on the left page and a biblical quote on the right. We had selected a symbol of an open book for their shared cemetery marker because it looked like a Bible.

Two years after my father's death I moved to Atlanta, accompanying my partner to a new job opportunity. My greatest grief was leaving my mother, though she had my brother and sister and grandchildren living nearby. My only consolation was that my mother understood, for she had followed the man she loved all the way to California, leaving behind her invalid mother in the care of her siblings and father. Whenever I had the occasion and resources to visit southern California, I would always stay a week, spending most of it with Mom rather than seeing my friends there. That, plus frequent phone calls, assuaged my guilt. My mom was the only member of my family to visit me in my Atlanta home, and she managed two visits in the years to come, even though she did not drive or fly. Once she came on the bus, and the other time I drove her cross country, and she returned by a train that departed out of New Orleans, affording us a visit to the French Quarter—a longtime dream of hers.

One fall when I was visiting her in the family home in North Hollywood, I decided to purchase her Christmas gift early. I had intended to send her new sheets and a comforter for the humble, full-sized bed that she and father had shared most of their lives, but realized the money I saved on shipping could go into the bedding itself. Plus, if she didn't like my selection, we could take it back to the store immediately. To my surprise, she liked my choices and did not resist the gift. I knew her predilection for laundering new things before using them, which, of course she did. As I helped her make up the bed with the freshly-laundered sheets, I noticed powder on the form-fitting bottom sheet and said, "Oh, Mom, it looks like some of the detergent didn't rinse out." It was then she explained to me that she always put my father's talcum powder on the mattress cover of the bed, and that's what was seeping through the fabric. She did this, she said, so the bed would smell like him. I was moved. As we proceeded to make up the bed, I discovered something else: she slept with a shirt he had worn under her pillow and his pajama top under his pillow because, after all these years, they retained his scent.

The novelist Marcel Proust devoted many words to the power of smell in recalling past experience. Earlier in this book I wrote of how mementoes may serve as sacramental time machines by which we travel back in time to past encounters with loved ones. As I write these words, I sip on coffee, whose aroma takes me back to mornings with Mom, who loved her coffee. It was because, growing up, I loved that smell of her coffee brewing that I learned to like its taste. And now coffee is a sacramental drink that unveils the memory of those homey, familiar times. For Mom, Dad's talcum powder and body scent combined to serve as a sacramental incense hallowing the sanctuary of their bedroom where they prayed together, on their knees, each night, and where they made love together behind their occasionally closed door. This was the bed on which I was conceived, and this would be the bed on which Mom would die early in 1999.

When my brother first called on that day in February, 1999, to ask if I had heard from Mom that day, I was immediately alarmed. I had spoken with her the night before, having made a brief call to her from my home in Atlanta as I was going out to see Hal Holbrook's traveling one-person show as Mark Twain. I asked her if she'd like me to call her when I got home and she said, no, she'd probably be on the phone with her sisters in Kansas, with whom she frequently had hour-long conversations. Our last words to each other were, "I love you." Later I would discover she had pulled out a book of Mark Twain sayings and, from the placement of the bookmark about 19 pages into it, she seemed to have "joined" me in the show in spirit by reading his witticisms.

The previous fall had given us warnings about her heart. I had managed to spend two separate weeks during the fall with her, and one time, as I was arriving from the airport, I found her getting ready, as my brother Steve was going to take her to the doctor. "What's the matter?" I asked. "I've had chest pains," she said simply, and continued making sure her beagle Schultze had enough water and food and papers on the floor by the back door. I was amazed the doctor had not wanted to see her immediately, but when my brother began recounting her symptoms to the doctor at her office, I had to add, "*And* she's been having chest pains!" "She didn't tell me that," Steve said, astonished. She was sent to a heart specialist who wanted to hospitalize her so as to regulate whatever medications he might prescribe. Yet he understood when she declined hospitalization, and did not force her. I couldn't help but think his own experience as an immigrant sensitized him to my mother's position. Having grown up with her own mother frequenting hospitals, and having witnessed our father's bouts with invasive surgeries, her phobia about medical help was deep. The tests showed she had had some kind of heart "event," and so was placed on a pharmaceutical regimen that would be monitored as an outpatient. That night in her house, I thought of spending the night to be on the safe side, though I usually stayed with friends nearby. But then I thought better of it. If she had had another heart event, what would I have done? Of course I would have called paramedics, who would have come with sirens wailing and paddles ready to shock her chest, frightening her and perhaps sending her to her death terrified. I had had enough experience with death to know that it is not the worst thing that can happen when the body is frail, tired, or ill.

It happened that, during one of those two fall visits, I had been invited to preach at a local church, and Mom came with me. The pastor, the Rev. Nancy Wilson, read that day's entry in my book of daily meditations to introduce me before the sermon. Synchronicity would have it that it happened to be a meditation about my mother. While working on the book, she had phoned me to ask me to include a meditation on Philippians 4:13, "I can do all things through Christ who strengthens me." My reflection was how this verse must have strengthened her in the crises of her life. Having this read before the congregation, being recognized and invited to stand, and receiving a prolonged ovation made my mother pleased and proud. And, given that so many in the largely gay congregation had non-accepting parents, her supportive presence lifted their hopes for their own parents.

In February of 1999 I visited again for another week of festivities surrounding my mother's 84th birthday. For one of these, she insisted on fixing the turkey herself. After I returned home to Atlanta, my mom called to ask me if I had caught Tom Brokaw's television special on *The Greatest Generation*, recounting the heroism and sacrifice of those who fought or supported the nation's efforts in World War II. "I'm glad our generation is finally getting the credit it deserves," she had said. A voracious reader, her eyesight was diminished by macular degeneration. But I had discovered large print books, and I sent her two for Valentine's Day, including Brokaw's book version of *The Greatest Generation*. Later I would find it on the end table beside her reading chair, the one that had been Dad's. She used it rather than the more comfortable recliner she had ordered for Dad, because the store had failed to deliver it before he died. The bookmark told me that she had gotten as far as page 160.

My brother called me back to tell me Mom was dead. As I wrote in an earlier chapter, I wanted to say, "You're kidding," knowing the mischievous sense of humor of both my brother and my mom. But I knew he was not, and I collapsed in the hallway of my house, wanting not to have heard the words, wanting somehow to undo the event. Apparently she had awakened that morning, taken a shower, put on a clean bathrobe, lay down on her bed and died peacefully, her hand on her heart. Her eyes were focused on the end of the bed, as if, my brother hoped, Dad had come to welcome her home. Or Jesus. Earlier I mentioned that if there were one public death I could undo, it would have been President Kennedy's. Now I write that if there was one personal death I could reverse, it would be Mom's. She loved me longer and better than any one on earth has or will do.

When I returned to Los Angeles, I told my brother and sister I would like to see Mom's body as soon as possible. My sister had joined my brother at the house before Mom's body had been taken away. I'm not sure why it was so important for me to see it immediately, but my sister and brother joined me and, as with Dick Hetz, Forrest Lawn brought her chilled body to us for a private viewing, before she was prepared and in a casket. I was struck by how beautiful she was even in death—old, yes, *and* beautiful.

She had already made it clear that she wanted her funeral to be identical to Dad's, including "Going Home" and me selecting and reading scriptures that suited her unique personality. I had also found and read during the funeral an unfinished letter to her family that Mom had apparently started in the fall after her first bout with her heart. It expressed concern that we all find faith, so we could be together again. I am the only one of the immediate family that still has ties to the church. We selected a coffin that had little flowers on its corners and made me think of her beloved film *The Sound of Music.* My brother, who had had the primary responsibility to watch out for her in her final years, persuaded us to select a double-strength vault, so protective of her fragile body was he.

Mom had told me about a young neighbor down the street. They had befriended one another, exchanging comments on and flowers from one another's gardens. She was Asian and did not speak much English, so when I happened upon her driving past her house, it took a moment before what I told her registered.

When she realized Mom was dead, she let out a frightening wail that was like those I had let out the night I learned the sad news. I was a little afraid other neighbors might think I was attacking her! The morning of the funeral, she left a little bouquet of flowers in a vase on the place on the front porch steps where Mom used to sit. When she came up to pay her respects to the open casket as the funeral concluded, she let out another wail. She gave voice to the deepest feelings we all suppressed, and I was grateful for her clarity.

In Mom's coffin, along with the scriptures I read at her funeral, and a copy of *Come Home!*, I placed a small ornate glass pitcher in her hands that I had brought her from Venice a few years earlier—a symbol of my being her vicarious traveler, taking overseas trips she never took but had always dreamed of. She had a vast pitcher collection, and, along with the letters my parents had exchanged, I retrieved some of the smaller pitchers I had given her over the years which would now serve for me as sacramentals of my mother's presence. Weeks later, when I returned to help clear out the house, I was given the task of going through her books—an estimated 2000 of them—for mementoes that she liked to place between their pages: family photos, postcards we had sent from far off places, news clippings, pressed flowers, etc. One envelope I recovered contained her own mother's obituary; on the envelope itself was a poem Mom had written in her memory. Two songs frequently played on the radio always remind me of the tears I shed while engaged in this task, Sara McLaughlin's "In the Arms of the Angels" and Eric Clapton's "Tears in Heaven," about whether his deceased child would recognize him in heaven. Months after that, I returned to help with a yard sale of the many things we didn't know what to do with, but each of which had a story or multiple stories that Mom could surely have told us. It's a lot easier clearing out sacramentals when you have no idea of their origin or meaning.

With both parents dead, it was all the more clear I was not getting out of this alive! Though stating the obvious, that death will take me too; living parents served as a buffer for me from such truth. Now that they're gone, I know my vulnerability in a deeper, darker, more certain way than before.

The Death of a Relationship

This grief would have been enough. But my grief was magnified by another death I was experiencing at the same time, the death of my "lifelong" relationship. The month before my mom's death, my partner announced that he was fantasizing about being single again. This was, I thought, the love of my life, the never-ending romantic movie, the one who swept me away from my family and home state, the one who insisted we have a marriage ceremony in our church, the one who wanted me to care for him if and when he developed AIDS. Because he was HIV-positive and I was not, I had not wanted to stand in his way when he had been offered the position of executive director of an AIDS agency in Atlanta, and he would not go without me, even though we had relatively recently re-established the relationship after he broke it off. At that earlier time of grief, I had gotten a massage, and enjoyed the epiphany that all those good feelings I had in my partner's presence resided within me, released now by the therapist's healing hands, independent of the relationship.

Moving to Atlanta was when we moved in together, first into an apartment, then into a house we bought together. Of the three homes under construction on a block in the Ormewood Park neighborhood of Atlanta, he wanted us to buy the biggest and showiest house. I pushed for the smallest and most modest house because it was within our budget, but also because I feared I might end up paying the mortgage all by myself were he to get sick. I had thought the only thing that would end our relationship would be his death. I believe he thought so too, and wanted me to care for him if he did get sick. But then the drug cocktail came along that offered the possibility of a longer life, and that was a game-changer for many couples, though we didn't think for us. An AIDS doctor started prescribing testosterone for him because lean body mass was believed to inhibit the wasting syndrome associated with AIDS, and this further affected his already apparent mood swings. I noticed he was spending more time on the internet, and I would hear AOL's "goodbye" whenever I neared him at his computer, as if he were hiding something. Addictive behaviors kicked in, I learned later, sexual and chemical. I write this as objectively as possible, not as "payback," because we are friends, who practice mutual forgiveness. He has already written about his experiences in a book and a blog and has become a self-described "poster-child" for crystal meth recovery.

At the time, however, my ideal world was shattered. It had been love almost at first sight, and even when I learned he was HIV-positive, I could not imagine letting a virus, even a death-dealing one, get in the way. After moving to Atlanta, almost every morning I had thanked God for the blessing of our relationship, our home, our supportive families, and our dog during my morning prayers on the deck of our Smurf-blue house, overlooking a kudzu-covered ravine with old trees rising toward the sky. My writing and editing career was flowing smoothly and at least some of our friends thought of us as a "power couple." He started writing at my encouragement, and wrote a book of which I was the first reader, as he was with several of mine. Early on our passionate relationship had been volatile and uncertain, but we had mellowed without losing the passion—or so I thought. I was totally satisfied, like Job in his wealth of family, friends, and lands. The AIDS cocktail I greeted as great news because it meant that we might extend our love decades ahead rather than mere years. He still had tension around the possibility that I might test positive, so much so that I never told him in advance when I was being tested. We practiced safer yet very intimate sex, and there were occasional intimacies or accidents when afterward I might think, oh, that might not have been a good idea. But I tried to keep such doubts to myself. And the relationship helped diminish the germ phobia I got from several relatives but had embellished on my own.

The premise of the relationship was that my partner might die, not the relationship. When we bought the house, I calculated how difficult it might become for him to navigate the staircase if he became ill. I brought with me from California a handsome carved cane I had bought for my father, just in case my partner might need it. I prepared myself for what I might need to do for him if and when he became less able to do for himself. Already I was bleaching his raw vegetables, killing bacteria that his immune-suppressed body might not be able to fend off. And of course I was making sure we ate a balanced, healthy diet. And none of this seemed a sacrifice. I had served in the "war" on AIDS, and done some demanding things, but nothing as demanding as this would be. It was my time to do this.

Henri Nouwen advised against comparing suffering. "Your

suffering is your own," he would say, "It doesn't help to compare your suffering to that of others." I quote this because I'm not certain which is the greater suffering: to lose a lover to death, or simply to lose a lover. In my case, I had been prepared to lose him to death. I had not been prepared to lose him to life, the extended life he now counted on with improvements of AIDS treatments. Whatever anger I experienced at his breaking off the relationship was overwhelmed by my grief.

I felt worse than unloved, I felt unlovable, unattractive, undesirable. Life now seemed like such a challenge that taking things "one day at a time" seemed like too big a chunk. It was "one thing at a time" for me: "Okay, I've completed this task. Now I will . . ." To get in touch with my foundations, I re-read books that had proven vital to my early formation, like *Zorba the Greek* and *To Kill a Mockingbird*. I re-read Nouwen's journal of unrequited love, *The Inner Voice of Love*, three times during my morning prayers. My recently-divorced former pastor gave me a copy of *How to Survive the Loss of a Relationship*, filled with commonsense coaching that proved helpful, such as "Don't call!" Many of us who suffer rejection think that if we could say one more thing or do one more thing for the beloved, they will return to us. Tain't so! Even though I had been given the old line, "It's me, not you!" I looked back at things I shouldn't have said, things I should have done differently. Something similar happens to those who suffer the death of a loved one, rehearsing the process that led to the death, thinking that if one thing had been done differently, the person would be alive.

My former pastor also gave me my mother's warning to us whenever we left the house, "Be careful." It's during times of extreme grief that relatively lesser troubles seem overwhelming— you know, the shoelace that breaks when you're in a hurry—and accidents happen. Three more friends died of AIDS that year. I worried if I would be able to keep my home or manage the bills that we had paid jointly. I endured a bad working relationship that threatened the greater part of my income. I dated people who turned out to be scary in one way or another. I drank too much. I acted out sexually. My car died on a busy interstate in downtown Atlanta in the middle of the night. Over the course of several months I had three flat tires. My wallet was stolen. The final insult came as I watched helplessly—despite my best efforts—as a fungus killed my lawn!

That year I scrutinized myself, and not just in relation to the death of the relationship. I considered also the death of my relationship with the church, called to ministry yet denied ordination because of my sexual identity. My hopes to reform the church remained, but I came to believe for the first time that it would not happen in my lifetime. If I had been straight or closeted or already ordained or simply less visible as a spokesperson for our movement, I might have been gainfully employed all these years, increasing my seniority and salary and benefits and retirement with each passing year, plus having ample time and income for study leaves and sabbaticals and vacations. As it was, I had little to show financially for all the speaking and writing and editing and ministry and unrelated jobs I had cobbled together over the years to survive. I am chagrined to say I began to look with envy at those whose heterosexuality or closet or prior ordination or minimal visibility afforded them more profitable positions and opportunities in church work. Underemployed men and women find it difficult to hold our heads high in a culture that not only views prosperity as a sign of worth, but advantages it. Even leaders of my own LGBT (lesbian, gay, bisexual, transgender) community treated me as deficient because I did not have the title "reverend," even though it was solely because I was out as a gay man. And younger people who were the beneficiaries of my and others' early activism seemed to have little idea or care for who we were and what we had done. In a dream I had, a colleague pushed me aside in favor of a new cause célèbre, saying "You're Old Testament!" implying the other was "New Testament." By my opponents I had been accused of being a "militant," while a leader in my own movement actually implied I was an "Uncle Tom."

I had already stopped going to church, but for broader reasons than my denomination's prejudices. It just wasn't working for me anymore. The worship experience no longer inspired me. It did not help me think. It did not make me wonder. I found my morning-prayer time much more helpful. I noticed a gnawing skepticism and cynicism growing within me by the second year after my great losses. My anger and impatience with the church and the government failing to recognize gay rights and marriages filled me with disgust for both. Saccharine-sweet people got on my nerves. I read most of Gore Vidal's books, reveling in his cynicism about American society and culture, amused by his cutting remarks about "sky-god" religions. I had been quite the optimist all of my life. I was becoming a curmudgeon. The Psalmist captured my experience:

> *My heart grew embittered,*
> *my affections dried up,*
> *I was stupid and uncomprehending,*
> *a clumsy animal in your presence.*
> *Even so, I stayed in your presence,*
> *you grasped me by the right hand;*
> *you will guide me with advice,*
> *and will draw me in the wake of your glory.*
>
> Psalm 73:21–24 (NJB)

"Even so, I stayed in your presence." In my morning prayer, I discovered something new in one of Jesus' parables, one that I had read dozens of times over the years and about which I had reservations. Jesus tells the story of a wedding feast to which the invited guests will not come. And I "heard" God saying to me, "Come in to the party." Let go of your negative feelings, however justified you may feel in having them. "Come in to the party." And that became my mantra whenever I sensed resentment, envy, bitterness, anger, or withdrawal bubbling up within me. I remembered also the elder brother whose father begs him to "come in to the party" celebrating his prodigal brother's return, and of the master who asserts his right to pay his kvetching servants equally though they were hired at different times of the day.

Believe it or not, this simple little phrase did much to get me over myself and into showing the proper reverence for the joy that is life, what the poet William Blake called "organized innocence" that can wonder at the world, play while experiencing suffering and addressing injustice, pray in the midst of distractions and disillusionment, achieve in the face of setbacks and failures, and love while enduring rejection and isolation. "Come in to the party" is another way of hearing "Repent, for the kingdom of God is at hand." This was and is the gospel Jesus and his followers proclaim in our better moments. "Come in to the party."

As I write this, I realize a comparable experience in college when I first came out, developed a severe case of mononucleosis, and felt abandoned by friends. On Christmas day in 1972 I was awake for only two hours, but a poem had come to me in my sleep that summed up my faith:

> Love is being crucified
> And rising again
> As if it never happened.
> That's love for you.
> That's love for *you.*

As I described in the previous chapter on Precipitous Death, a near-death experience may give a taste of the peace or wisdom or enlightenment that may come in the actual death experience. Extreme grief is a near-death experience. It's standing on the edge of one's own grave. It taught me that I don't stand there alone, and that when I take the final step I will not be alone. But it has also taught me to turn from the precipice as I am able, while not denying it's there. Just as my friend Scott Rogo observed that my first book contained crucifixions followed by resurrections, so death leads me to a life qualitatively different from what it had been. Only in this new life did I begin a new relationship that has continued until this day, as well as a renewed vocation in interim ministry, though not in my home denomination. I like the metaphor of the latter—in essence, all ministry is "interim" or "temporary," just as life is.

The Death of Calvin

None of this or all of this prepared me for the one death to date for which I am directly responsible. Growing up, my brother's dog regularly bit me, terrorizing the back yard and making it off-limits as a playground for me. I was sad when Freckles got out of the backyard and was hit by a car, dying a day later, but I retained my fear of dogs. Eventually I overcame my fear or rather, learned to control my fear, because I believe dogs react to fear. I came to be friends with Smokey, a retriever belonging to a friend from church with whom I boarded in college. But I did not become a "dog person" until my then partner and I adopted a Golden Retriever/ Labrador mix from the Atlanta Humane Society. We named him Calvin for the Reformed theologian, John Calvin. In a sense, we grew up together, the child in me and this puppy bonding in such a way that I finally understood why so many people called dogs "man's best friend." And I did not fear him when he grew to be over one-hundred pounds! Calvin enjoyed chasing weeds when I was gardening, and swimming in the pond of the Carter Library, when that was still allowed. And he loved to fetch his ball. Calvin had a happy face, with a big grin and sparkling eyes, and he loved to sleep with us on the bed or on the sofa.

From California my mother's dog, a beagle named Schultze, "wrote" Calvin a letter to which he "responded," and it occurred to me that Calvin was teaching me in his own way a philosophy that differed much from his namesake. We began a collaboration on a book we initially called *Calvin's Philosophy*, translated from the Canine by me. Over a glass of wine at an American Academy of Religion gathering in New Orleans, I told my then editor, Stephanie Egnotovich, about Calvin's book. To my surprise, she was excited and wanted to see it. It helped that she, too, was a dog person. Within weeks, we were offered a contract for the manuscript. I explained it wasn't quite finished. And Stephanie said, "By all means, add to it as you want."

Calvin got the first hardbound book in the family, as all my other books till then had been published as trade paperbacks. The publisher renamed it *Unleashed: The Wit and Wisdom of Calvin the Dog* by Calvin T. Dog and wanted to accompany the text with illustrations. I would have preferred actual photographs, but agreed to send a few "select" photos to the illustrator—as it turned out, fifty photos in all! Jim Kelley captured Calvin's spirit in his illustrations, working through his grief at the death of his own two dogs earlier that year. Calvin was one of two authors Westminster John Knox Press featured at the Chicago Book Expo that year. The publisher flew us up to Chicago and put us up at a different (and as it turned out, nicer) hotel than where its staff was staying because it allowed dogs. Calvin was the first dog to be allowed on the floor of the Expo, Lassie having been denied the previous year. He took his turn "pawtographing" books at the same table where Charlton Heston had just finished signing copies of his autobiography. We had made a rubber stamp of Calvin's paw print, and I mimicked his scrawl using the hand I do not write with. As we later ascended the stairs of the famed Navy Pier for the gala reception hosted by the book distributor Ingram, a security guard pointed to Calvin and said, "No dogs!" I explained, "But he's an author!" To which the guard replied, without hesitation, "Oh, he's okay, then."

When my partner and I separated, I fought for custody of Calvin. Calvin was my solace in the death of my relationship and the death of my mother, licking my face whenever I cried or sobbed, trying to make me feel better. His ministrations discredited for me the 12th century Christian teacher Abelard's notion that compassion was the one thing that set us off from other creatures. I am willing to agree with Abelard that compassion is the emotion that makes us one with God (his version of "atonement"), but I am unwilling to say other creatures do not have this capacity. Calvin was also the one who set boundaries for my personal life. I would not leave him alone at night. Anyone who wanted to get close to me had to at least be friendly to Calvin. Calvin's presence in my life filtered out undesirables.

On a walk around Grant Park, Calvin and I noticed a dog that apparently had been abandoned running back and forth across a street. I knew I would be heartsick if I returned to find her hit by a passing motorist. Territorial Calvin wouldn't let me get near her, so I took him home and came back with a collar and a leash but, unthinkingly, no alluring treat. So I sat down on a slope in the park as she circled me at a distance, coming closer and closer with every pass, looking at me with her sad, lost eyes. Finally she came close enough to place the collar and leash on her. She had adopted me, and after fruitless weeks posting signs of a lost dog, I adopted her, naming her Hobbes, after the tiger in the comic strip, because she bounced with his energy. Calvin accepted her into the family. I told him she would be "his" dog! She too was part golden Lab, and looked like Calvin's sister, though smaller at 70 pounds.

Years later, Calvin developed an unrelenting limp, and x-rays suggested bone cancer. His compassionate veterinarian, Dr. Gail Kearney, shared tears with me as she explained the diagnosis, and thought he might have a month to live. He lived a year and a month past the diagnosis. By then we were living in San Francisco. I was on temporary assignment there as an interim pastor, and Calvin gave me my first story in the pulpit. The day before we were to fly there, he devoured almost wholly a thousand-page Bible concordance, which lists scripture references by key words. I was able to joke with the congregation that when we arrived in the Bay area, he was still "exegeting" scriptures all over the place! We had found a furnished townhouse to rent from a fellow dog lover near Lake Merced and near the doggy beach, Fort Funston. Calvin and Hobbes had an opportunity to go to the beach for the first time, and also enjoyed walking down to the lake. Calvin could walk less and less, and his shoulder area swelled larger and larger. A vet from our Atlanta clinic now practiced in San Francisco, and it was good to bring him for care to a familiar and friendly face.

I had to begin walking Calvin and Hobbes separately, as Calvin could not walk so fast nor so far. Sometimes I would simply bring them out to the huge grassy lawn beside the complex where Calvin would sit happily, and Hobbes would sniff out gophers. One Christmas, as I was preparing the house for my partner's visit from Atlanta, Calvin tumbled down the staircase from the bedroom and never went upstairs again. I began sleeping downstairs occasionally with Calvin so he wouldn't be alone, me on the sofa and him and Hobbes on their doggy beds.

One day Hobbes accompanied me to the laundry room in another building while Calvin lounged on the lawn behind the house. As we returned, we found Calvin had found his way around our building, crossed the street, and headed toward the building where we were! His eyes beamed brightly, as if to say, "Look what I could do!" I was amazed he had come so far in so short a time to find us.

But eventually, one night, he could not manage to make it up the two steps to the back door of the townhome. He kept falling over. No amount of encouragement or prodding could persuade him and he lay helpless on a concrete slab outside for the night— and the next several nights. I wrapped him as warmly as I could and tried myself to sleep outside with him, but it was bone-penetrating cold. One night it rained, and I borrowed a collapsible table from the laundry room and used a plastic shower curtain to construct a kind of tent to shield him. I had already put in "the call" to a vet who would come to the house to euthanize him, but he couldn't come for two days. If I left Calvin's sight he would moan, and if I tried to go upstairs to work in my bedroom/office, he would wail. So I rearranged my schedule to stay by his side. In his final hours, he lay quietly as I talked with him about all we had done together, how much I loved him, and how happy he had made me. When the vet finally came, he agreed with my evaluation of the situation. He explained that he would give Calvin two injections. The first might cause him to behave atypically until it took effect, and I should keep my distance. The second would take his life. I had already spoken with the vets in Atlanta and San Francisco about what I should do with Hobbes during this time, deciding to allow her the run of the place as we proceeded.

Calvin fought the first injection, requiring me to put a comforter over his head to avoid being bitten. Then he lay there, and, since I was not to get too close, I started talking to him again. As is my wont, given my profession, I included the attending vet in the conversation, and asked him if he had any faith system. As it turned out, he was raised by Holocaust survivors who had no use for God. This was a hard conversation to turn from to adequately care for my dog, and I regretted bringing it up. Finally the first injection took effect, and I lay down on the ground next to Calvin, his eyes looking straight into mine as I stroked the top of his head. The doctor told me he would not close his eyes when the second injection took effect, but in fact, he did. He closed his eyes as if going to sleep. I can't remember the order, but his breathing stopped, his heart stopped, and he was gone. I wailed like a banshee and threw myself on his body like a Mediterranean widow-woman. A fellow pastor had asked if I wanted her there, and I was grateful but I declined. The reason was my whole life I've taken care of other people's feelings and in this moment I did not want to edit my feelings or my actions or my grief for fear of upsetting another. As it was, I think I frightened the vet, and he asked if I was all right. I said I would be. At the same time, my dog-loving neighbors watching next door decided to get to know me, and we became fast friends for the rest of my stay.

The doctor pronounced Calvin dead, and I cut a lock of his hair for safekeeping. The vet put him in a "body bag" that looked suspiciously like an ordinary Hefty bag, and we included one of his favorite little yellow footballs he loved to fetch so it could be cremated with him, transmuting both into the eternal realms as the ancients believed. The vet had to move his truck closer and left me with Calvin while he did so. I carried the bag myself to the front door, crying, sobbing, and wailing all the way because I could feel Calvin's body heat through the bag. I lifted it myself into his truck, to the amazement of the doctor. And I learned firsthand how much heavier dead weight seems. I keep his ashes today in our bedroom in a pine box with another of his little yellow footballs on top. If I am buried, his ashes will be placed inside the coffin with me. Even in death, we will be fighting for bed space! To date, our thirteen years together was the longest uninterrupted intimate relationship I have had in my adult life. He had slept on my bed almost every night until he could no longer jump up

I am not given to visions, and I suspect people who are. And I don't think what I saw the following Sunday morning was a vision, but real, and yet such an amazing experience of synchronicity to actually reveal something transcendent—at least to me. I was walking Hobbes before I had to leave for church. My gaze was distracted from her, but I felt her tug on the leash in greeting and I looked down and saw Calvin at my feet. At least it looked just like Calvin, but he was young and energetic and playful and happy. And his fur was not golden as before, but shimmering silver white. I had never seen such a dog before and he had no collar. He walked along with us—really *bounced* playfully alongside us—so, believing him to be lost, I tried to encourage him to come into our courtyard to give him food and water, as well as giving me an opportunity to call and alert the complex's security so the owner might be found. Hobbes was amenable to his presence, which was also intriguing. But as I began to close the gate, he bolted and ran off. I went after him, but he seemed to have vanished, and I never saw him again. I thought we would cross paths in the weeks or months to come if he belonged to anybody in the complex, but that never happened. I chose to take it as a sign, though its significance I hesitate to guess. I want to believe that it revealed that somewhere Calvin was happy, without the limitations of old age, arthritis, and bone cancer. In my heart, in my memories, Calvin is always happy and will always be. I had never been so close to death, close enough to be its cause, choosing to euthanize him. And yet I had never been so close to life, so full of the life that Calvin and I shared, full of joy at his existence. I wonder if my absolutely intense involvement in his death made me less doubtful of death's need to punctuate life.

Epilogue
My Own Death

Like many young people, I once thought I would die young, perhaps even sacrificially, saving someone or standing for something. Now nearing sixty, dying young is hardly possible! I also thought that death would be when others would truly appreciate me, as I described when I began this book, because that was what I witnessed played out in dramas, novels, and my own life experience. Even awful people were suddenly regarded as saints; the dull as interesting; the gifted or loving as tragically undervalued. From time to time it was as if I could hear an echo when I did something kind, or funny, or outstanding: "He was so kind—I remember the time when he . . ." "He had a keen wit—he once said . . ." "He made an outstanding contribution to . . ." I pointed out in the first chapter that the root words of "eulogy" mean "good words," and I think it a shame that we save our good words about someone until after he or she can hear them.

Seminarians are sometimes assigned to write about what they imagine their funerals will be like. Apparently, many have rather grandiose expectations, because afterward, they are invited to write more realistically about what is *likely* to take place. I think of it as a less demanding Christian version of Buddhist monks contemplating a decaying corpse to obtain a visceral and certain understanding of mortality. "Day by day remind yourself that you are going to die," Saint Benedict urged in his rule for contemplatives. I earlier alluded to the existentialist philosopher and novelist Sartre viewing death as a sacrifice of self-definition, when others take complete control of you, making of your life as they wish. Perhaps that's partly why my first book was autobiographical, taking charge of how I might be remembered. Later I came to understand that recounting one's personal history, no matter how honest the attempt, involves a certain "fashioning," if not a little unintentional fiction or fantasy, given the unreliability of personal memory and objectivity.

After attending the funeral of a colleague during which I was horrified by the selection of one of his eulogists—one who had made himself the enemy of the departed in life, no matter how grandly he spoke of him in death—I came home and wrote out my own funeral plan, including as eulogist the friend I wrote of earlier, who disliked eulogists who talked about character defects in the deceased. I had once chanced a remark to John Boswell that I didn't want people to feel inordinately sad at my passing, and he commented that I could do something about that, so I included uplifting hymns and songs that reflected the gravitas of the moment without playing on its melancholy, ending as the postlude a song from Disney's *Song of the South*, "Zip-A-Dee-Doo-Dah," something that would leave attendees with a song in their heart and a smile on their lips. An occasionally campy gay friend who died of AIDS did something similar at the end of his staid Presbyterian memorial service by requesting Abba's song "Dancing Queen" as the postlude.

As is my wont, I wanted to keep my service to an hour, so I included no invitation for people to share personal stories— as was then popular during many of the funerals I attended or led—causing awkward silences, an inordinately long service, and the occasional sobbing-grandstanding of someone who wasn't particularly close to the departed but loved the attention. If people had stories to tell, let them do it in a social setting, a wake before or a reception after. San Francisco Bishop James Pike's friends gathered a month after his death for cocktails and storytelling, and that had appealed to me. Funerals are, in my view, an occasion to worship (literally, to "shape worth"), giving God thanks or simply giving thanks for a person's life.

I also believe a funeral or memorial service should be about the one who is dead. I am less concerned about using it as a platform to recruit for the person's cause than I am about using it to proselytize for a particular faith. After all, funerals in apartheid South Africa became a rallying cry for freedom when other mass gatherings were banned by the government. But during a recent funeral I attended the pastor asserted that only Christians will get into heaven, a questionable view best left unexpressed in moments of grief. At one AIDS funeral in southern California, a Presbyterian pastor shocked the surviving family and friends by declaring the young man was now in hell for his sins.

Growing up, as I have said, I disliked pastors beginning eulogies with the disclaimer, "I didn't really know this person . . ." because to me it implied judgment for not attending their church. Over the years I have discovered the importance of interviewing surviving family and friends to put together a coherent reflection of the person's character and interests. This process also gives survivors opportunities to feel their loss as they tell stories about the loved one, stories they may readily share one-on-one when they might find a larger audience intimidating. This was particularly helpful when I led the funeral of a much beloved nine-year-old who died of leukemia, possibly the most difficult eulogy I ever gave. After one memorial service, someone came to me asking me to do hers when the time came, explaining she liked the way I talked about the departed. She had recently attended her aunt's funeral in which her aunt's name was only mentioned once!

On my fiftieth birthday I met with a "pre-bereavement" counselor to plan my own "final arrangements." I think the employees of the mortuary were a bit shocked to see someone who looked young and healthy doing so, but I had taken to heart my family's discussion when selecting my father's casket about how we should each pick out our own and save others the trouble. But I also wanted to remind myself on such a significant birthday—a half-century—that I too will die. The counselor was very kind and helpful and responsive to my concerns about cost. As we talked, I was brought coffee in a silver pot on a silver tray that also held a porcelain coffee cup and saucer. The showroom had rather pricey models, but the catalogue contained cheaper alternatives. The casket I selected was made of dark wood, European in style, and cost about $1700. The counselor offered to bring one up from the storeroom for me to inspect, and when I balked at the pinkish lining, questioning its appropriateness for a male, he corrected my misunderstanding, explaining that such a color brings out the flesh tones in a complementary way. He held the fabric to my skin, and I joked, as if considering a new piece of clothing, "Can I pull this off?"

Whereas the mortuary, part of a large chain, required no prepayment of any kind for its "before need" services, the cemetery was another matter. My family owns plots in the cemetery, and I thought I'd give it the business of "opening the grave," as well as purchasing the vault and marker there. What first disturbed me was that their cheapest but no less effective vault was not in their miniature display of models that cost twice as much or more, a model that had not been offered in burying either of my parents. Then, having recorded my choices, the counselor asked how I would like to pay for this, meaning *now*. When I undoubtedly looked surprised, she said, "Oh, we have an installment payment plan with low interest." Fascinated with this scheme, I asked, "Why would I pay interest on a service I haven't yet received?" She didn't quite "get" what I was driving at, though I imagine she said something about it "fixing" the price. But I pursued it further. "And why would I prepay for a service I might not get to use—say, if I died in a plane crash or in another country? Anyway, the money for all this would probably have to come out of my house." She was not to be derailed in making her sale, declaring, rather indiscreetly, "We expect cash at the time of the burial." "I'm sure you'll take a credit card," I replied. Still pushing, she said, "Well we can't keep your file unless you prepay." I said, "Then just put what I've selected in my parents' file." She was not happy with this. Nor was I happy with her.

Until my mother's burial at that cemetery nearly two years earlier, I had thought to be cremated, a choice my mother did not like. Now I found myself wanting to be alongside my parents in death, a kind of comfort burial, as "psychorational" (my own word) as comfort food. A decade later, I have begun reconsidering cremation, largely because of cost and convenience. Adding to my awareness of mutability, however, the original site I had selected for my ashes to be poured out has itself been cremated—a hillside beside a green wooden cross overlooking Santa Barbara on the grounds of Mt. Calvary Retreat House where I had occasionally taken retreat, but destroyed in the Montecito fire of the fall of 2008.

I had told a friend I wanted her to assist my partner in tossing the ashes over the hill, wryly warning her that I had heard ashes were sometimes hard-packed and she might want to bring an ice pick.

Yet I had chosen cremation long ago as a "second best" choice, wanting, as I did, to be one with the earth. My true wish has always been to be buried straight into the ground, to be absorbed into the soil. With the advent of green burials, that is now possible in many states, including my home state of California and my present state of Georgia. So that, too, is a possibility.

Whatever is done with my body, I want a party. As a youth I had mentioned this, and my parents thought it odd. But it really was part of their tradition as well: the potluck meal provided by relatives, neighbors, friends, and church members that usually followed one of our family funerals was remarkably cheerful and fun and comforting. In Atlanta I participated in a New Orleans-style celebration of a friend, parading on his street with parasols behind his urn and a Dixieland jazz band playing "When the Saints Go Marching In." We swaggered across a bridge to the two-story lobby of a brick building that housed his and others' lofts. Large round tables were filled to overflowing with Popeye's chicken and "fixins" and desserts and, naturally, an open bar. But the most appealing fantasy for my celebration I discovered in Japanese director Kurosawa's amazing, concluding segment of his film *Dreams*, in which a colorful musical procession wends its way through a village, joyfully bearing the body of a beloved citizen to its final resting place. Okay, so now I'm in the place of those seminarians having to depict what may actually happen following my death!

The truth is, I may have already experienced my Kurosawa parade, having served as a grand marshal of Atlanta's Pride parade on November 1, 2009. It was an honor to be recognized for a lifetime of work and writing. But as I proudly waved to partiers along the parade route, I was mindful that one of two surviving family members of my parents' generation was on her deathbed in a small town in Kansas. That week I would give her eulogy and follow her body in a very different kind of parade, the motor cortege to the cemetery. I was deeply moved at how cars on either side of the road came to a complete stop until we passed, some switching on their headlights in solidarity, even a rough-looking biker on a Harley. Workers along the street took off their hats and placed them over their hearts. Catholics made the sign of the cross.

Unaccompanied by a police escort, we went through stop signs and red lights and busy intersections without a car or honk interrupting our flow. Tears of pride came to my eyes. Proud to have my aunt so honored, though anonymously, proud of small town civility, proud of the human spirit that can—in its best moments—show respect to a fellow, fallen human being.

Death, and contemplating my own death in particular, have, above all, taught me gratitude. Gratitude for each moment of my life, the good and the bad, that has shaped my soul into who I am today. As a youth I saw this summed up in three words on a marker covering a mausoleum niche that holds the cremated remains of the actor and comedian Ed Wynn, a version of which will be on my own marker. It is a bas-relief letter with his signature upon which is written,

Dear God:
Thanks!